DISSERTAT
REVIEW SPRINT

Finish & Defend Your Chapter in 30 Days—Powered by AI

DISSERTATION LITERATURE REVIEW SPRINT

Finish & Defend Your Chapter in 30 Days—Powered by AI

Rafiq Muhammad, MD, MIHMEP, Ph.D.

Disclaimer

No part of this book is to be duplicated, shared, or transmitted in any manner without explicit written authorization from the author. This prohibition extends to all forms of reproduction, whether by copying, recording, or using any mechanical or electronic means, as well as storing or retrieving information through any system. While certain segments of this book have benefitted from advanced AI tools, extensive human intervention in the form of editing and revising has been undertaken to ensure its precision, clarity, and reliability.

Notice of Liability:
It is vital to acknowledge that the information provided in this book comes with no explicit guarantees. The author cannot be held accountable for any losses or damages that may arise from the content or links contained in this text.

Websites and links
Given the ever-evolving nature of the internet, websites and their content are subject to continual changes. The hyperlinks referenced in this book are intended solely for informational purposes. The author does not warrant the accuracy, reliability, or any other aspects of the content found on external websites linked within this book.

ISBN: 978-91-990413-0-8

Imprint: Muhammad Rafiq

TABLE OF CONTENTS

THE COMPANION COURSE

This book gives you the full roadmap to write a high-quality literature review chapter in 30 days. But if you'd like **additional structure, accountability, and guided feedback**, you don't have to navigate this journey alone.

To support you further, I've created a **companion course** that brings this sprint to life—with video walkthroughs, templates, AI toolkits, writing trackers, and peer community support.

What You'll Get in the Companion Course:

- **Video lessons** to accompany each chapter of this book
- **Customizable templates and planning boards** for searches, synthesis, and structuring your review
- **AI integration tutorials** (ChatGPT, Zotero, Consensus, and more)
- Direct feedback and Q&A
- **Access to a writing sprint community** of fellow graduate students
- **Lifetime access** with updated tools, examples, and bonus modules

Whether you need **motivation, mentorship, or just a clear starting point**, this course gives you the structure and support to finish your literature review—faster, better, and without burnout.

Who It's For:

This course is designed for:

- Master's or PhD students writing their literature review
- Researchers overwhelmed by scattered notes, tabs, and half-finished drafts
- Students who want to work smarter using ethical, AI-powered research tools
- Anyone who wants structured daily goals and momentum

Enroll or Join the Waitlist

If you're reading this during launch week, enrollment may already be open. Otherwise, you can join the waitlist for the next live cohort.

https://www.gradsummit.com/dissertation-literature-review-sprint

This book gives you the system.

The course gives you the **coaching, tools, and community** to finish the job.

Let's finish your literature review—together.

A 30-DAY TRANSFORMATION FOR PHD RESEARCHERS

Pursuing a PhD is often described as one of the most intellectually fulfilling experiences of a lifetime—and one of the most emotionally and mentally demanding. Beneath the prestige and promise of academic discovery lies a complex journey filled with uncertainty, isolation, and relentless pressure. Many students begin the doctoral process with ambition and enthusiasm, only to find themselves wrestling with questions they never anticipated:

How do I structure a literature review that actually supports my research?

Every PhD student knows the weight of the literature review chapter. It's the backbone of the thesis, the intellectual scaffolding for your research, and—far too often—the place where progress stalls. You open ten tabs, download a hundred PDFs, and still feel like you're going in circles. The question you're supposed to answer feels vague. The mountain of papers feels insurmountable. Days slip by with little to show but scattered notes, half-read abstracts, and growing anxiety.

You're not alone. Thousands of doctoral candidates around the world struggle with the same paralysis at this stage. The problem isn't a lack of intelligence or effort—it's a lack of structure, feedback, and focused momentum. Traditional advice on writing a literature review is often abstract or overwhelming. Worse, it rarely integrates the AI tools that can dramatically speed up your search, synthesis, and writing process.

This book offers a different path. Designed as a structured, 30-day sprint, it guides you step by step from a blank page to a fully written, properly cited, and submission-ready literature review chapter. Along the way, you'll use cutting-edge yet accessible tools—like ChatGPT, Zotero, and Recite—to enhance your research process without compromising academic integrity.

This book is designed as a 30-day sprint—each "Day" serves as a self-contained, action-oriented unit that builds upon the last to guide you from a blank page to a fully written, submission-ready literature review chapter. Unlike traditional textbooks, it blends structure, motivation, and real progress into manageable daily chunks. You can follow it sequentially over 30 days to build momentum, or adapt the pace to your schedule—focusing on the sections where you need the most support. Each Day includes focused guidance, writing tasks, AI tool recommendations, and workflow tips to help you move from confusion to clarity with purpose and confidence. Whether you're stuck, overwhelmed, or just getting started, this book is both a system and a companion for writing your literature review faster, smarter, and with academic integrity.

Here's how the transformation unfolds:

- **Days 1–5 (Define & Discover)** help you define your research question, build smart search terms, and navigate databases with AI-assisted precision.
- **Days 6–10 (Organize & Evaluate)** show you how to collect, organize, and critically evaluate sources, using concept maps, matrices, and skimming frameworks to move from chaos to clarity.
- **Days 11–17 (Write the Review)** guide you through writing every section of your review—from introduction to thematic synthesis to conclusion—anchored in structure and scholarly voice.
- **Days 18–25 (Polish & Finalize)** sharpen your citations, flow, formatting, and self-editing using digital workflows that cut down on busywork.
- **Days 26–30 (Transition & Reflect)** bridge your literature review to your methodology chapter, keep you motivated, and prepare your draft for submission—while reinforcing sustainable habits for the next phase of your thesis.

The result? A professional-grade literature review chapter and the skills to tackle every other part of your thesis with more confidence, efficiency, and clarity. By Day 21, you'll have a complete literature review draft. Days 22–30 guide you through revising, formatting, and linking to the methodology chapter so you can hand in a committee-ready, defendable manuscript.

This book is more than a how-to manual—it's a cognitive map, a writing coach, and a daily accountability partner. Whether you're stuck at the start or halfway through your review, this sprint will get you unstuck, moving forward, and proud of your progress.

So take a deep breath and let's start transforming your PhD journey—one focused step at a time.

WHO SHOULD READ THIS AND WHAT YOU WILL GAIN

You sit down at your desk with determination, your laptop open to a blank document and a growing list of articles cluttering your browser tabs. Your supervisor expects a literature review chapter draft in a few weeks, but instead of clarity, you feel paralyzed. You've gathered dozens of PDFs, highlighted hundreds of passages, and taken pages of notes—but how do you actually turn all this into a coherent chapter?

You type a few lines and quickly delete them. The narrative feels flat. The structure isn't clear. "Should I organize this chronologically, thematically, or methodologically?" you wonder. You read another review paper for inspiration, but the process only makes you feel more overwhelmed.

A notification pops up on your phone: a reminder to meet your advisor next week. Panic creeps in. "What if I don't have anything substantial to show them?" you whisper to yourself.

You're not alone. Thousands of graduate students across the world wrestle with the same challenge: writing a literature review that is comprehensive, focused, well-structured—and done on time. It's not a matter of intellect or effort. It's about missing a roadmap, a system to follow, and practical guidance that bridges the gap between gathering literature and producing academic writing.

That's exactly what this book delivers.

Dissertation Literature Review Sprint is your step-by-step guide through the most overwhelming phase of your thesis. Whether you've just started collecting sources or are stuck with piles of disconnected notes, this 30-day sprint offers a focused, AI-powered path from uncertainty to clarity. You'll learn how to search, synthesize, organize, and write your literature review chapter with confidence—and finish it in just one month.

Each day builds on the last, blending cutting-edge tools like ChatGPT, Zotero, Rayyan, ResearchRabbit, and Consensus with proven academic strategies. You'll move from chaos to structure, from scattered thoughts to scholarly narrative—all while maintaining your voice and academic integrity.

This book is for you if:

- You're working on a master's or PhD thesis and need to write a literature review.
- You've collected sources but aren't sure how to organize or synthesize them.
- You want to write faster and smarter using AI tools responsibly.
- You feel overwhelmed, stuck, or under pressure to produce your first draft.

Whether you're just starting or need to regroup and refocus, this sprint will equip you with practical systems, motivational structure, and clear daily wins to keep you moving forward. You don't need to be perfect—you just need a plan. This is it.

WHAT YOU WILL LEARN

Each day comes with clear goals, reflective tasks, and optional AI tools to accelerate your progress—without compromising on academic quality.

This book will teach you how to:

- **Define a Clear Research Question**
  Use AI and scholarly frameworks (PICO, FINER, SMART) to clarify and sharpen your topic.
- **Build a Powerful Keyword and Search Strategy**
  Develop Boolean search strings and AI-enhanced strategies to retrieve relevant, high-quality literature efficiently.
- **Organize and Manage Your Research Library**
  Set up a streamlined, tag-based, and AI-synced literature management system using tools like Zotero, Rayyan, and ResearchRabbit.
- **Critically Evaluate and Synthesize Sources**
  Skim with purpose, paraphrase ethically, and code findings into themes using concept maps and synthesis matrices.
- **Write with Structure and Confidence**
  Draft your chapter step by step—introduction, thematic sections, contradictions, and conclusion—using prompts, templates, and real examples.
- **Edit, Cite, and Polish with Precision**
  Apply layered revision, AI-assisted editing, and reference management to finalize a submission-ready chapter.
- **Bridge to the Next Stage**
  Link your literature review to your methodology chapter, prepare for committee feedback, and plan your next thesis milestones.

ABOUT THE AUTHOR

Rafiq Muhammad, MD, MIHMEP, Ph.D., is a data scientist, health policy specialist, and doctoral graduate of the Karolinska Institute in Sweden. He also holds a Master's degree in International Healthcare Management, Economics, and Policy from SDA Bocconi in Italy. Dr. Rafiq brings over a decade of experience in healthcare research, academic publishing, and student mentorship.

He is the author of several bestselling academic books under the *Mastering Research* series, including *Research Design Simplified, Literature Review Simplified,* and *Write and Publish A Scientific Paper.* His work bridges rigorous academic training with practical, AI-enhanced research workflows that empower students and scholars worldwide.

Dr. Rafiq is passionate about demystifying the research process for graduate students. Drawing from his own experiences and the challenges his mentees frequently encounter, he created this sprint model to transform the way literature reviews are written—faster, smarter, and with clarity.

Whether you're a first-time thesis writer or a returning researcher navigating academic writing under pressure, his tools, systems, and teaching will help you write with purpose—and finish with confidence.

Mastering Research Series

This book is part of the *Mastering Research: Design, Execution, and Publishing Made Simple* series—an essential collection authored by Dr. Rafiq Muhammad. This all-in-one series offers step-by-step guidance, real-world strategies, and practical tools tailored for each stage of the research process. The series includes: **1. Research Design Simplified**, **2. Literature Review Simplified**, **3. Research Proposal Writing Simplified**, **4. Write and Publish Scientific Paper**, **5. PhD Journey Simplified**, and **6. Qualitative Data Analysis with ChatGPT and QualCoder**. Together, these books provide a complete roadmap—from formulating your first research question to confidently publishing your findings.

Literature Review Simplified: A Practical Guide for Beginners (Mastering Rese...	Literature Review Simplified: A Practical Guide for Beginners Second Edition ...	Research Design Simplified: A Beginner's Guide to Qualitative, Quantitative, ...	Write and Publish Scientific Paper: A Step-By-Step Publication Guide For Begi...	Research Proposal Writing Simplified: A Step-by-Step Guide to Research Propos...	Qualitative Data Analysis With Chatgpt And Qualcoder: A Step-By-Step Guide To...
Buying Options	Buying Options	Buying Options	Buying Options	Buying Options	Buying Options
★★★★½ 32	★★★★½ 17	★★★★★ 64	★★★★½ 10	★★★★★ 7	★★★★½ 14

Scan to order on Amazon

PART I: DEFINE AND DISCOVER

Day 1: What Is A Literature Review—And Why It Matters

Starting a PhD journey is both intellectually exhilarating and deeply demanding. Among the many milestones along the way, few loom as large—or feel as daunting—as the literature review chapter. It's the part of your thesis where you're expected to demonstrate not just what you know, but how deeply you've immersed yourself in the scholarly conversation surrounding your topic. And for many graduate students, it's where momentum slows and self-doubt creeps in.

This book is designed to change that.

Over the next 30 days, you'll follow a structured, AI-enhanced sprint that transforms the literature review from a vague obligation into a purposeful, progressive writing experience. But before we dive into tools and techniques, let's begin by asking the most fundamental question: What exactly is a literature review, and why does it matter so much in a PhD?

Reframing the Literature Review

At its core, a literature review is a scholarly synthesis of existing research on a particular topic (1–3). It's not a summary of articles, nor a bibliographic list—it's an analytical narrative that traces what's known, what's debated, and what remains unresolved (4). A good literature review identifies key theories, evaluates methodological trends, pinpoints research gaps, and sets the stage for new contributions.

If you're writing a thesis, your literature review has a specific function. It doesn't just sit alongside your research—it justifies it. It explains why your study matters by demonstrating how it emerges from, and contributes to, the existing body of knowledge. Unlike a standalone review article, which offers a comprehensive overview for its own sake, a thesis-integrated review supports your central research question. It is the intellectual scaffolding that allows your argument to take shape.

And yet, despite its importance, the literature review is often the chapter that paralyzes students the most. Why? Because it's structurally ambiguous, cognitively overwhelming, and time-intensive. You may open dozens of browser tabs, download hundreds of PDFs, and still feel like you're spinning in circles.

The Common Struggles—And a New Solution

If you've ever felt lost inside a mountain of academic papers, you're not alone. Common struggles include:

- **Information overload**—You find too much, not too little.
- **Unclear scope**—You're unsure what belongs and what doesn't.
- **Perfection paralysis**—You wait to start writing until you've read "everything."
- **Tool fatigue**—You bounce between reference managers, databases, and note apps, unsure what's working.

Traditional advice often exacerbates the problem: "Start broad and narrow down." "Read widely." "Map the field." All true—but not all helpful when you're under time pressure, lacking structure, and unsure how to organize your thinking.

That's where this sprint model, paired with responsible use of AI tools, makes the difference.

Let AI Handle the Chaos—So You Can Think Critically

This book doesn't promise shortcuts—it offers smartcuts. We won't bypass academic rigor, but we will eliminate unnecessary bottlenecks using AI in ways that preserve integrity while boosting efficiency.

Here's how your AI toolkit will help:

- **Perplexity** will help you understand how your topic is framed in current research using natural-language queries and cited summaries (5).
- **Consensus** will surface claims from peer-reviewed literature that are supported (or contradicted) by evidence—especially useful for health and social sciences (6).
- **ResearchRabbit** (7) and **Connected Papers** (8) will allow you to explore the literature graphically, identifying clusters, debates, and key nodes.
- **Elicit** (9) and **Scholarcy** (10) will generate structured summaries of PDFs and extract key variables, helping you review papers faster.
- **Zotero** (11) (especially when enhanced with ZoteroGPT) will manage your references, annotate PDFs, and sync citations seamlessly into your writing.
- **scite.ai** (12) will flag whether a paper is widely supported or challenged by subsequent research—an important signal when weighing credibility.

These tools won't replace your scholarly judgment, but they will free up your cognitive bandwidth so you can focus on critical analysis, synthesis, and writing.

A 5-Step Roadmap to a Submission-Ready Review

The structure of this 30-day sprint is grounded in a five-phase process. Think of this as your map through the forest:

1. **Define your topic and scope** – Clarify your research question, frame your focus, and understand how others are discussing it.
2. **Search and discover** – Build a smart, Boolean-enhanced search strategy using both academic databases and AI recommenders.
3. **Analyze and organize** – Skim effectively, extract key findings, and visualize thematic patterns using maps and matrices.
4. **Write and synthesize** – Draft your review section by section, integrating AI-generated prompts where helpful but writing in your own scholarly voice.

5. **Reflect and revise** – Polish your draft, enhance flow and citation accuracy, and ensure the narrative aligns tightly with your thesis goals.

We'll take each of these stages in turn—one per week, more or less—and break them into smaller, daily tasks. Each day's progress compounds. By the end of the sprint, you won't just have a draft; you'll have a chapter that demonstrates intellectual mastery and strategic thinking.

Using AI Ethically and Transparently

As AI becomes more integrated into academic workflows, ethical questions naturally arise. Here are three non-negotiable guidelines we'll uphold throughout this book:

- **Always verify** - If an AI tool provides a summary, statistic, or citation, go back to the source PDF to confirm accuracy.
- **Always cite** - Give credit to both the original study and, where appropriate, the AI tool that assisted you—especially in the methods section or footnotes.
- **Always protect** - Do not upload confidential, or unpublished material into public-facing AI tools.

Think of these principles not as constraints, but as scholarly habits that will serve you well throughout your academic career.

Your First Action Step

Let's close this chapter with a few foundational tasks that will carry forward into the rest of your sprint.

1. Define Your Topic in Plain Language

Write a two-sentence explanation of your research topic as if explaining it to a curious friend outside your field. Example:

"My research explores how different online teaching strategies influence student motivation in higher education. I'm particularly interested in how structured vs. flexible course formats affect engagement."

When you sit down to define your topic, imagine you're describing it over coffee to someone who has never set foot in your field. Strip out any discipline-specific jargon and focus on two things: **what** you're investigating and **why** it matters. To get you started:

- **Identify the core idea.** Ask yourself: "What is the single phenomenon, relationship or problem I'm exploring?"
- **Translate key terms.** For each technical phrase, find an everyday synonym. For instance, "instructional modality" becomes "teaching style."
- **Frame your angle.** Why does this matter? Who benefits from knowing the answer?
- **Draft two sentences.** The first should state *what* you're studying; the second should explain *why* or *how* you'll look at it.
- **Refine for clarity.** Read it aloud—does it still sound clear? If your curious friend asks "But what exactly will you do?" your next draft needs to be even sharper.

Now it's your turn—grab a blank page, follow these steps, and nail down your topic in plain language before you dive into the literature.

2. Run an AI Recon

Open **Perplexity** or **Consensus**, enter your topic as a query, and note the top three peer-reviewed papers it cites. Save their titles and URLs—you'll use them again soon.

For example, "How do structured versus flexible online course formats affect student motivation in higher education?"—and let it surface the top three peer-reviewed papers. Copy each paper's title, first author, year, and DOI or URL, then save these details in a simple spreadsheet. These three key studies will anchor your search, help you refine keywords, and guide your deeper literature review.

3. Draft a Starter Keyword List

Open ChatGPT (13), and type a prompt like "Suggest search terms and synonyms for [your topic]". Review the suggestions and add at least five useful terms to your research notebook.

Open ChatGPT and enter your two-sentence topic—e.g., "Suggest search terms, synonyms, and related concepts for: How do structured versus flexible online course formats affect student motivation in higher education?"—then scan its suggestions for terms that cover your core concepts (like "structured learning" or "flexible instruction"), your population ("higher education students"), and your outcomes ("motivation," "engagement"). Refine any that seem too broad or narrow, pick at least five strong keywords, and save them in your research notebook—optionally grouping them into categories such as Concepts, Population, Methods, and Outcomes—to fuel your deeper literature searches.

4. Reflect on AI Use

Write a short reflection (≈100 words) on one benefit you observed while using an AI tool—and one potential risk. Be honest. This will help build awareness as we go.

Looking Ahead

Congratulations—you've transformed a daunting first step into a clear, actionable foundation for your literature review. By defining your topic in plain language, running an AI recon to surface core studies, drafting a focused keyword list, and reflecting on AI's benefits and risks, you've sharpened your purpose, equipped yourself with the right tools, and begun building the research vocabulary that will guide every chapter to come.

In the next chapter, we'll refine your research question using classic scholarly frameworks (like FINER, PICO, and SMART) combined with AI-assisted ideation. The clearer your question, the more targeted your search will be—and the faster your review will come together.

Take a deep breath. You've made an excellent start.

Day 1 Summary Box

- A literature review is a critical synthesis that frames your research within existing scholarship, highlighting key debates, gaps, and contributions.
- Common challenges include information overload, scope confusion, and tool fatigue—often leading to stalled progress.
- AI tools such as Perplexity, Consensus, Elicit, Scholarcy, and Zotero support search, synthesis, and citation—but must be used ethically and transparently.

Day 2: Sharpening The Spear—Refining Your Research Question With AI

If the literature review is the backbone of your thesis, then your research question is the spine's first vertebra. Everything aligns from here.

Today's chapter is about precision. You may have a broad area of interest—"climate policy," "digital education," or "mental health"—but that's not enough. What you need now is a tightly focused research question that will guide your entire literature review process: from keyword searches to source selection, thematic coding, and synthesis. Without that clarity, every AI tool you use will generate noise instead of signal.

Fortunately, AI can do more than assist with skimming and summarizing—it can also help you ideate, test, and refine your core question. When used strategically, it becomes a brainstorming partner, a quality checker, and even a methodological advisor.

Let's dive in.

From Umbrella to Laser Beam: Why Focus Matters

Imagine your initial topic as a wide umbrella—broad, diffuse, and inclusive. That's a good place to start. But to conduct a meaningful literature review, you need to close the umbrella and sharpen it into a focused spear: a specific, researchable, and relevant question that reflects both your academic intent and the scope of existing literature.

Take the topic "social media and mental health," for example. It's broad enough to cover thousands of papers across disciplines. But it's not yet actionable. What kind of social media? Which population? What mental health outcome? A more refined version might be:

"How does daily Instagram use affect anxiety levels in college students?"

Now we're getting somewhere. It's specific, testable, and aligned with real-world data sources.

Using AI to Generate and Test Research Questions

One of the most powerful—and time-saving—ways to accelerate this process is by enlisting the help of AI. Today, we'll use a trio of AI tools to move from fuzzy to focused in under an hour.

1. Perplexity (Deep Research Prompting)

Start by asking Perplexity to suggest three measurable, recent, and novel thesis questions on your broad topic. Use prompts like:

"Suggest three specific, measurable thesis questions on 'social media and mental health'. Cite recent peer-reviewed studies (2023–2025)."

This prompt works well because Perplexity returns cited outputs you can verify immediately. Check the DOI links and see if the papers align with your interests.

2. ChatGPT

Paste your topic into ChatGPT, Elicit or Anthropic's Claude (14). These AI tools use Natural Language Processing to analyze top abstracts and generate research questions based on patterns found in the literature. It often includes variables, populations, and research angles you might not have considered.

Run your research question through ChatGPT and ask it to evaluate the question using both the PICO (15) and FINER (16) checklists. This will help you assess its clarity, feasibility, and methodological strength—ensuring the question is well-structured before moving forward. This dual-layer review ensures both conceptual soundness and methodological rigor.

- **FINER** - Is the question Feasible, Interesting, Novel, Ethical, and Relevant?
- **PICO** - Does the question define Population, Intervention, Comparison, and Outcome?

These filters ensure that your question isn't just clever—it's usable.

The outcome will typically look like a structured response that breaks your question down into:

- **PICO:**
  - **P (Population):** Who the study focuses on
  - **I (Intervention/Exposure):** What is being introduced or examined
  - **C (Comparison):** What the intervention is compared against (if applicable)
  - **O (Outcome):** What effects or results are being measured
- **FINER:**
  - **Feasible:** Is it doable given time, resources, and expertise?
  - **Interesting:** Is it compelling to the investigator and the field?
  - **Novel:** Does it add something new to the existing literature?
  - **Ethical:** Can it be conducted ethically?
  - **Relevant:** Does it matter to science, policy, or practice?

Together, this feedback will help refine your question into something researchable, relevant, and methodologically sound.

3. Consensus (Check if the Question Has Already Been Answered)

Paste your candidate questions into Consensus to see whether existing literature supports or contradicts the underlying claim. This protects you from unknowingly choosing a question that's already been settled—or already debunked.

Safety Reminder - Always open the cited PDFs and verify. AI tools are fallible. A hallucinated citation can derail your credibility.

Selecting the Strongest Candidate

By now, you should have a shortlist of 2–3 research questions. But which one is best? Use a simple decision matrix: score each question from 1 to 5 on each FINER and PICO criterion.

Criteria	Guiding Question	✓ / ✗
F - Feasible	Can the study be completed with available time, skills, resources, and access to data?	
I - Interesting	Is the research question engaging to the researcher and important to the field?	
N - Novel	Does it provide new knowledge, confirm prior findings with better methods, or challenge existing understanding?	
E - Ethical	Can the study be conducted in accordance with ethical standards and obtain necessary approvals (e.g., IRB)?	
R - Relevant	Will the outcomes have academic, clinical, policy, or social significance?	

FINER Scoring Template

Criteria	Guiding Question	Score (0–5)	Comment / Justification
Feasible	Is the study practical given time, expertise, funding, and data access?		
Interesting	Will this study engage researchers and the field?		
Novel	Is the question original or a meaningful replication/improvement?		
Ethical	Can the study meet ethical guidelines and obtain necessary approvals?		
Relevant	Will it contribute meaningfully to science, policy, or practice?		
TOTAL (out of 25)			

PICO Scoring Template

Component	Guiding Prompt	Score (0–5)	Description / Notes
Population / Problem (P)	Is the target population or problem clearly defined and specific?		
Intervention / Exposure (I)	Is the main intervention or exposure clearly described and measurable?		
Comparison (C) ***(if applicable)***	Is the comparison condition or group clearly stated?		
Outcome (O)	Are the outcomes well defined, measurable, and relevant?		
TOTAL (Out of 20)			

Selecting the most promising research question requires more than intuition—it demands structured, comparative judgment. That's why you've applied the FINER and PICO frameworks, scoring each shortlisted question against critical criteria like feasibility, novelty, and outcome clarity. But how do you assign those scores?

Start by interpreting the scores as a sliding scale of confidence and specificity:

5 = Strong alignment (e.g., clear, specific, well-supported, realistic)

3 = Moderate (e.g., partially defined or somewhat achievable)

1 = Weak or unclear (e.g., vague scope, uncertain methods or ethics)

0 = Criterion not met at all

Ask yourself: Do I have enough clarity and evidence to justify a high score? If not, give a lower score and make a note in the "Comments" column explaining why. This process doesn't just rank your questions—it forces you to critically assess gaps in planning and conceptual clarity.

By learning how to evaluate and justify your scores, you're already thinking like a researcher—clear, critical, and systematic.

Once you've selected your top-scoring question, copy it into your digital research notebook and into your Zotero library's "Notes" field. You'll refer to it constantly from this point on. If you're using ResearchRabbit, use this final question—or three seed papers related to it—to begin mapping your citation network. In the next chapter, you'll use this same question to generate your keyword architecture.

Why This Step Shapes Everything Else

Refining your research question isn't just about narrowing your focus. It's about aligning every downstream decision:

- Search terms
- Database filters
- Article inclusion criteria
- Thematic synthesis
- Methodological frameworks

A question that's too vague leads to a literature review that's directionless and bloated. A question that's too narrow might leave you without enough material. The ideal research question sits in the sweet spot—broad enough to matter, tight enough to be tractable.

AI helps you locate that sweet spot faster—and with greater confidence.

Sprint Task: Today's Core Tasks

To lock in your learning and build momentum, complete the following tasks before the next day's sprint.

Manual Tasks

1. **Write your umbrella topic**
   Example: "Social media and mental health"
2. **Refine it into 2–3 specific research questions**
   Example: "How does daily Instagram use relate to anxiety in college students?"
3. **Assess clarity and scope**
   Check: Is it measurable? Is it population-specific? Can it be answered through a review of literature?

AI-Enhanced Tasks

Step	Task	Tool	Deliverable
1	Brainstorm 3 candidate questions	Perplexity	Copy-paste top 3 with DOIs
2	Evaluate questions	ChatGPT (FINER + PICO tools)	Create a simple table scoring each
3	Choose one and justify	Manual	Write 100-word rationale
4	Sync to Zotero & ResearchRabbit	Zotero, ResearchRabbit	Save note and capture concept graph screenshot

Sample reflection: "I chose this question because it balances feasibility with novelty and opens space for comparative analysis between platforms. Consensus showed limited conclusive evidence, suggesting room for further review."

Quick AI Prompts

Perplexity Prompt

"Act as a graduate supervisor. Suggest 3 novel, measurable research questions on 'social media and mental health'. Cite at least two 2024–2025 peer-reviewed papers per question."

ChatGPT Prompt

"Evaluate this question using FINER and suggest improvements: How does daily TikTok use influence anxiety among first-year university students between 2023–2024?"

Final Thoughts: Clarity Is a Compass

It's tempting to skip this step—to dive into databases and start searching before your question is truly ready. But that's how students end up with disconnected summaries instead of a coherent narrative.

A well-crafted question is more than an anchor—it's a compass. It keeps your sprint grounded, your AI tools aligned, and your energy focused. In the chapters ahead, you'll turn this single sentence into a systematic search strategy and a structured outline for your review.

But for now, sit with it. Shape it. Challenge it. Let it guide your thinking.

Next, in Day 3, we'll use that question to brainstorm a rich vocabulary of keywords and Boolean operators that will supercharge your academic search engines.

Your literature review is about to gain momentum.

Checklist: Selecting a Focused and Researchable Question

Dimension	Criteria	Check
I. Conceptual Clarity and Focus	Specifies population, phenomenon, and context	[ ]
	Free from vague or overly broad terms	[ ]
	Answerable through literature (not primary data collection)	[ ]
	Appropriately scoped for a dissertation chapter	[ ]
	Aligned with thesis aims or problem statement	[ ]
II. Methodological Soundness (FINER)	Feasible: Can be addressed within available time and resources	[ ]
	Interesting: Relevant to the field and intellectually engaging	[ ]
	Novel: Addresses a gap, offers new angle, or improves prior studies	[ ]
	Ethical: Does not involve sensitive or inappropriate topics for secondary research	[ ]
	Relevant: Findings have potential academic, clinical, or policy significance	[ ]
III. Structural Strength (PICO)	Population: Clearly defined target group	[ ]
	Intervention/Exposure: Specific concept being examined	[ ]
	Comparison (if applicable): Logical control or reference condition	[ ]
	Outcome: Measurable, relevant results or variables	[ ]
IV. AI Support and Verification	Generated candidate questions using AI tools (e.g., Perplexity, ChatGPT, Elicit)	[ ]
	Checked question relevance using Consensus or academic databases	[ ]
	Verified the question has not already been conclusively answered	[ ]
	Reflected on the benefits and risks of using AI in the ideation process	[ ]
V. Final Review	Scored and compared using FINER and/or PICO frameworks	[ ]
	Selected the strongest question with clear rationale	[ ]
	Saved final question in your research notes, Zotero, and/or ResearchRabbit	[ ]

Day 2 Summary Box

- A focused, well-formulated research question is essential for guiding your entire literature review—from search strategies to synthesis and structure.
- AI tools such as Perplexity, ChatGPT, Elicit, and Consensus can assist in generating, testing, and refining research questions quickly and effectively.
- The FINER and PICO frameworks provide a structured method to evaluate candidate questions for feasibility, clarity, novelty, and relevance.
- Selecting the strongest question through scoring and reflection ensures your review remains targeted, coherent, and methodologically sound.

Day 3: From Concepts to Keywords — Building Your Literature Search Arsenal

With your research question now crystal clear, you're ready to equip yourself with the vocabulary that will unlock the literature you need. The mission is straightforward but foundational: transform your focused research question into a rich set of keywords and search phrases. This is how we turn inquiry into discovery.

Search engines, databases, and AI-powered literature tools are only as effective as the words you feed them. A well-constructed keyword strategy will help you retrieve not just more studies—but the *right* studies. It reduces irrelevant noise, reveals hidden connections, and ensures that your final review isn't just comprehensive but *credible.*

What used to take hours of manual brainstorming can now be accelerated through natural language processing, semantic mapping, and entity extraction—thanks to modern AI tools. So let's build your academic search vocabulary one layer at a time.

Keywords Are Not Just Words—They're Strategy

At first glance, keywords seem simple. They're just the terms that represent the key concepts in your research question, right?

Yes—but with nuance. Effective keyword design involves:

- Identifying **core concepts**
- Generating **synonyms and related terms**
- Incorporating **controlled vocabulary** (like MeSH)
- Mapping **concept clusters**
- Formatting into **Boolean search strings**

Take this research question as an example:

"How does daily Instagram use affect anxiety levels in college students?"

This question contains at least three core concepts:

- Social media platform (Instagram)
- Psychological outcome (anxiety)
- Target population (college students)

But those three ideas can be expressed in dozens of ways across disciplines. A psychology database might use "psychological distress" or "mental health," while an education journal may refer to "student well-being" or "academic stress." That's why Day 3 is all about expanding your vocabulary—smartly and systematically.

Step-by-Step Keyword Expansion with AI

Let's walk through a five-step workflow that combines your human judgment with machine intelligence.

Step 1: Start with Your Seed Concepts

Break your research question into 3–5 core ideas. These often align with the PICO elements you mapped on Day 2 (Population, Intervention, Comparison, Outcome).

Example seed terms:

- *Instagram*
- *Anxiety*
- *College students*

Write them down, then ask: "How else might these be described in academic literature?"

Step 2: Use AI to Generate and Enrich

Here's where AI becomes your co-pilot.

- **ChatGPT** - Paste your research question into ChatGPT and ask: "Can you help me generate synonyms, acronyms, and related search terms based on this research question?" You'll receive a curated list of relevant terms, which you can organize or expand based on your specific databases (e.g., PubMed, Scopus). Optionally, ask ChatGPT to format them as a CSV-style table for easy export and review.
- **MeSH on Demand** (from the National Library of Medicine) - Paste in your research question or an abstract from a related article. This tool suggests Medical Subject Headings (MeSH)—the standardized vocabulary used by PubMed. These terms ensure your searches align with how databases *index* knowledge, not just how authors phrase it.
- **litsearchr** (for R users) - If you're comfortable with R *(a powerful and widely used programming language and free software environment for statistical computing and graphics)*, **litsearchr** is a powerful, reproducible tool for building systematic search strategies (17). Instead of relying solely on manual keyword brainstorming, litsearchr uses **text mining and keyword co-occurrence networks** to identify key terms used in the literature.

  To begin, you upload **2–3 seed articles** that are closely aligned with your topic. The tool then performs a **co-occurrence analysis**, identifying words and phrases that tend to appear together across those texts—especially within titles, abstracts, and keywords. This helps surface terminology you might otherwise overlook, such as technical synonyms, related constructs, or emerging buzzwords.

  litsearchr then outputs:

  - A **Boolean-ready search string** containing structured combinations of the terms using AND/OR logic.

- A **co-term network graph**, which visually shows how frequently terms appear together, helping you identify clusters of related concepts or potential subtopics.

  This approach enhances **comprehensiveness** and **objectivity** in keyword selection, especially for systematic reviews, scoping reviews, or meta-analyses. Plus, it supports **transparent and replicable search strategy development**, which is increasingly expected in high-quality evidence syntheses.

- **TextRazor** can identify niche concepts (like anxiety scales, demographic labels, or even intervention names) by parsing full text or abstracts (18).

Key tip: Don't just collect terms—curate them. Not every suggestion will be relevant.

Step 3: Cluster and Validate with Recommender Graphs

Once you've drafted a robust list of terms, upload them into **Connected Papers**.

This tool visualizes how papers and concepts are connected, helping you identify:

- **Core clusters** (where research is dense)
- **Outlier terms** (that may belong to another field)
- **Synonym gaps** (terms you didn't think to include)

If, for example, adding "Snapchat" instead of "Instagram" suddenly expands your graph, you've uncovered a conceptual link worth exploring. This process turns your keyword list into a *living, evidence-backed search vocabulary*.

In addition to Connected Papers, you can also use **ResearchRabbit** to deepen and visualize your literature landscape. Once you've selected 2–3 seed papers aligned with your research question, upload them into

ResearchRabbit to generate **citation and co-authorship graphs**. These graphs go beyond static keyword lists to reveal real-world research linkages and intellectual clusters.

ResearchRabbit helps you:

- **Spot core clusters** – Highly interconnected papers that represent foundational research in your area.
- **Identify emerging topics** – Newer studies with lower citation counts but high relevance, ideal for spotting cutting-edge directions.
- **Uncover interdisciplinary bridges** – Linked papers outside your initial field that share authors, citations, or themes, pointing to adjacent disciplines or concepts.

For example, if your seed paper focuses on "TikTok and anxiety," and the graph surfaces a related but separate node on "algorithmic content exposure," you may discover a critical new lens for your literature review or conceptual framework.

This process **validates your current direction** and **expands your thinking**, turning a short list of known papers into a **living, evolving citation map**—ready to guide your search terms, thematic structure, and inclusion criteria.

Step 4: Build Boolean Search Strings

Now it's time to translate your terms into search logic.

Use **OR** to link synonyms (broadens results), **AND** to combine different concepts (narrows results), and **quotes** for exact phrases. A well-built Boolean string might look like:

```
("Instagram" OR "social media" OR "digital platforms") AND
("anxiety" OR "psychological distress" OR "mental health") AND
("college students" OR "university students" OR "young adults")
```

Want to go further? Use truncation (e.g., *anxiet* to catch *anxiety, anxieties*), field tags (e.g., *tiab* for title/abstract), and proximity operators (e.g., *NEAR/3*) for more advanced control in databases like PubMed, Scopus, or IEEE Xplore.

Step 5: Save, Sync, and Version Your List

You're building a *search protocol*—not just a one-off query. Treat it as such.

- Save your master list in **Zotero** (explained in detail in Day 5 sprint) as tags or in a note.
- Upload to **Rayyan** (explained in detail in Day 5 sprint) for future screening (19).
- Save versions as you iterate: "Keywords_v1.txt", "Keywords_v2_MeSH.txt", etc.
- Consider syncing to a Google Sheet if working collaboratively.

This attention to detail pays off in reproducibility, transparency, and systematic review standards like PRISMA.

Ethical Considerations and Quality Control

AI makes keyword generation faster, but not always smarter. Before you finalize your terms:

- **Preview them in a database**: Do they retrieve relevant studies?
- **Watch for homonyms**: Terms like "engagement" or "stress" can mean different things in different fields.
- **Document the date and tool used**: This helps track changes over time—especially important for formal protocols.

Remember: *AI helps you brainstorm, but you remain the scholar.*

Sprint Task: Build Your Keyword Arsenal

Today's deliverables will fuel your database dive in Chapter 4. Set aside about 45–60 minutes to complete the following.

Manual Tasks

1. **List your core concepts**
   - Example: Instagram, anxiety, college students
2. **Generate 2–3 synonyms for each**
   - Instagram: "social media," "digital platforms"
   - Anxiety: "stress," "psychological distress"
   - College students: "undergraduates," "young adults"
3. **Draft Boolean search phrases**
   - Example: "Instagram AND anxiety AND college students"
4. **Save your list**
   - Name your file: *Keywords – Social Media and Anxiety.txt*

AI-Enhanced Tasks

Task	Tool	Deliverable
Generate search terms	ChatGPT	Export CSV of ≥15 terms
Extract controlled vocabulary	MeSH on Demand	Screenshot of top 10 MeSH terms
Text-mine two seed PDFs	litsearchr or TextRazor	Co-occurrence graph or keyword list
Build Boolean string	Manual or litsearchr	Boolean-ready string
Validate with ResearchRabbit	Import 3 articles	Screenshot with new synonym added

Quick AI Prompts

- **ChatGPT**:
  "Generate synonyms, abbreviations, and related MeSH for: daily TikTok use AND anxiety in university students."
- **Perplexity**:
  "Suggest a Boolean search string using tiab field tags for PubMed combining these terms: [paste list]."

Final Thoughts: Your Keywords Are Your Compass

The work in this chapter might seem technical, but it's profoundly strategic. Every keyword you define is a door into the literature. Get the vocabulary right, and you'll retrieve the highest-quality sources with minimal wasted time.

More importantly, your list will evolve. As you begin searching, you'll discover new terms, eliminate off-topic ones, and fine-tune Boolean expressions. That's the mark of a living literature review—adaptive, expansive, and intelligently scoped.

In the next chapter, we'll put this vocabulary to work. With your keywords in hand, we'll explore how to search smarter—not harder—across academic databases using AI-enhanced filters and visual tools.

Let's get ready to dive into the data.

Checklist: Developing a Comprehensive and Search-Optimized Keyword Strategy

Dimension	Criteria	Check
I. Identify Core Concepts	Broke down the research question into 3–5 key concepts (e.g., platform, outcome, population)	[ ]
	Clearly aligned each concept with PICO elements where applicable	[ ]
	Avoided vague terms; ensured concepts are specific and researchable	[ ]
II. Generate Synonyms & Variants	Used AI tools (e.g., ChatGPT, Elicit) to generate synonyms, acronyms, and related terms	[ ]
	Identified MeSH or controlled vocabulary terms (e.g., via MeSH on Demand)	[ ]
	Used text-mining tools (litsearchr, TextRazor) to extract co-occurring terms from seed articles	[ ]
	Evaluated the relevance of AI-suggested terms (did not include generic or off-topic ones)	[ ]
III. Visual and Network Validation	Mapped related terms using ResearchRabbit and/or Connected Papers	[ ]
	Identified interdisciplinary overlaps or overlooked clusters	[ ]
	Expanded the keyword list based on validated conceptual links	[ ]
IV. Construct Boolean Search Strings	Grouped synonyms with OR, concepts with AND, used quotes for phrases	[ ]
	Included truncation symbols and field tags for advanced search (e.g., *anxiet*, tiab)	[ ]
	Tested search string in at least one database (e.g., PubMed, Scopus, Lens.org)	[ ]
V. Save and Document Strategy	Saved keyword list and Boolean strings in Zotero, Notion, or a versioned document	[ ]
	Named and versioned files clearly (e.g., "KeywordList_v1.txt")	[ ]
	Uploaded keyword sets to tools like Rayyan for future screening	[ ]
VI. Ethical and Quality Controls	Verified AI-generated terms in the context of actual academic usage	[ ]
	Avoided homonyms or ambiguous terms that may distort results	[ ]
	Documented the tools, date of generation, and rationale for term inclusion	[ ]

Day 3 Summary Box

- A clear research question must be translated into a robust, structured keyword strategy to retrieve the most relevant and credible literature.
- Effective keyword construction includes identifying core concepts, generating synonyms, using controlled vocabularies (e.g., MeSH), and formatting Boolean search strings.
- AI tools such as ChatGPT, MeSH on Demand, litsearchr, TextRazor, Connected Papers, and ResearchRabbit enhance keyword discovery, mapping, and validation.
- Boolean logic (AND, OR, quotes, truncation) is used to construct reproducible, database-optimized search strings that reduce noise and increase precision.

Day 4: Smart Searching — Finding the Right Literature with AI and Precision

Now that you've developed a strong research question and built a robust, multi-layered keyword list, it's time to launch your literature review search. Today's mission is deceptively simple: enter your search terms into the right tools and begin harvesting relevant academic literature.

But here's the truth: just typing keywords into Google Scholar or your university library won't cut it.

Graduate-level research requires a smarter, more strategic search—one that combines traditional academic databases with cutting-edge AI search engines, recommender tools, and visual mappers. The goal isn't just to find *papers*. It's to discover **relevant, high-quality, diverse perspectives** on your topic, fast—without drowning in thousands of PDFs.

This chapter will show you how to set up a lean, intelligent, reproducible pipeline for academic discovery. Let's begin.

Why Search Strategically?

Most students struggle not because there's a lack of literature—but because there's *too much*. The key isn't to read more—it's to read better.

A well-structured search does three things:

1. Surfaces **high-impact, relevant** sources.
2. Filters out **noise and redundancy**.
3. Evolves over time—bringing new literature to you automatically.

To make this happen, we will combine **AI-enhanced discovery tools** with **discipline-specific databases**, layered with automation and visual filtering. Think of it as moving from flashlight to floodlight.

Match the Right Tool to Your Research Domain

Not all databases are created equal. Each field has preferred platforms, indexing styles, and citation architectures. Choose your primary search tools based on the type of evidence you're after:

Need	Best Tool(s)	Why
Fast cited claims	**Consensus**	Shows peer-reviewed claims with citations
Cross-discipline overview	**Semantic Scholar**	Includes AI-generated 1-line summaries
Medical depth	**PubMed (Advanced Search)**	Supports MeSH + Boolean precision
Engineering & CS	**IEEE Xplore**	Proximity and phrase control (e.g. NEAR/3)
Psychology & social sciences	**PsycINFO**	Deep indexing and thesaurus terms
Citation analytics	**scite.ai**	Flags whether papers are supported or disputed
Massive global index	**Lens.org**	Spans 250M documents, API-ready

Start by picking 2–3 that best suit your field and get familiar with their advanced search syntax. You'll be copy-pasting Boolean strings across these tools shortly.

Launch Your AI-Enhanced Boolean Queries

Remember that carefully structured Boolean string you built in Chapter 3? Now's the time to use it.

Paste into Major Databases

Start with **PubMed** or **Scopus** and paste your Boolean string directly. You can refine results using:

- **PubMed field tags**: title/abstract[tiab], NOT review[pt]
- **Scopus syntax**: TITLE-ABS-KEY() + proximity (W/3)
- **IEEE Xplore operators**: NEAR/3, ONEAR/2

Precision, Not Overload — Advanced Search Strategies for High-Impact Results

By now, you've launched your first full-scale literature search. You've built Boolean strings, tested multiple databases, and begun organizing a core stack of relevant sources.

While beginner searches help you cast a wide net, advanced search strategies help you fish in the right waters. Our aim is no longer just to gather papers—it's to **curate a high-quality, comprehensive, and transparent evidence base** that will support your review and stand up to academic scrutiny.

Welcome to the precision stage of your literature sprint. Let's refine what you've found, enhance your queries with smarter syntax, and use AI tools to catch what standard keyword searches often miss.

Why Basic Search Isn't Enough

Even the best keyword list won't uncover every relevant paper if your search strategy isn't adaptive. Here's why:

- **Terminology drifts**: "Anxiety" might appear as "psychological distress," "nervousness," or "mental strain."
- **Concepts scatter**: Related ideas are discussed across disciplines using different language.
- **Important papers get buried**: Traditional databases prioritize recency or citation counts, not relevance to *your* topic.

Advanced search techniques help you cut through this complexity using Boolean logic, proximity operators, semantic indexing, and citation networks.

Supercharge Your Boolean Strings

Let's start with what you already know: **AND** narrows results, **OR** broadens them, and **NOT** excludes.

But now it's time to add nuance:

Proximity Operators

These allow you to search for terms that appear *close together*, which often signals conceptual linkage.

- **Scopus**: W/3 (within 3 words)

```
TITLE-ABS-KEY("Instagram" W/3 anxiety)
```

- **IEEE Xplore**: NEAR/3
- **Lens.org**: NEAR/2

Field Tags

Focus your search on titles and abstracts—where key ideas are concentrated.

- **PubMed**: [tiab]

("Instagram"[tiab]) AND ("anxiety"[tiab]) AND ("college students"[tiab])

- **Scopus**: TITLE-ABS-KEY()

Wildcards and Truncation

Catch spelling variants or related word forms:

- instagra* → Instagram, Instagramming
- anxiet? → anxiety, anxieties

These refinements allow your search to remain both broad in recall and sharp in relevance.

Chain the Citation Network

When you find one good paper, don't stop there. Use it as a launchpad to uncover *related* studies—both foundational and cutting-edge.

- **ResearchRabbit** - Upload seed papers and let the graph evolve. Weekly digests alert you to new, high-similarity publications.
- **Connected Papers** - Enter a DOI and explore visual maps of co-citation and thematic drift.
- **scite.ai**: Reveals whether citations in a paper are *supporting*, *contrasting*, or *neutral*—helping you triage for evidence strength.

This is how you **move laterally** in the literature—surfacing overlooked but important work.

Apply Filters Strategically

Filters are powerful—but they should be your **final step**, not your first.

Recommended filters (applied post-export):

- **Date range**: Last 5 years (e.g., 2019–2024)
- **Document type**: Journal articles only

- **Language**: English (or relevant to your field)

Start broad, then slice down. Avoid premature filtering—many valuable papers use unexpected phrasing and might be excluded if your initial net is too tight.

Test with AI Meta-Search Tools

Run the same string through **Consensus** and **Perplexity**. These tools may:

- Surface synonyms you didn't consider
- Flag trending or recently cited papers
- Show terminology drift across fields

Any useful new terms or papers? Add them to your master keyword list and citation tracker.

After you've built an initial Boolean search string, it's time to **stress-test** and **enhance** it using AI-powered meta-search tools like **Consensus** and **Perplexity**. These platforms combine natural language processing with vast scientific databases to return not just matching documents—but semantically relevant results, even when terminology varies.

Why This Step Matters:

Traditional search engines rely heavily on **exact keyword matches**, which means valuable studies using slightly different terminology can slip through the cracks. AI meta-search tools reduce this risk by:

- **Interpreting meaning**, not just string matching.
- **Synthesizing across disciplines**, where the same concept might be described in different ways.
- **Prioritizing recency and impact**, so you spot emerging terms and high-value papers.

What to Do

1. **Paste your Boolean string** or main research question directly into platforms like Consensus and Perplexity.
2. Skim the **top results** and pay attention to:
    - **Synonyms and alternate phrasings** that you haven't yet included (e.g., "emotional distress" vs. "anxiety").
    - **Emerging terms** or **newly cited papers**—especially those from the past 12–24 months.
    - **Terminology drift** across fields. For instance, the term "algorithmic exposure" might appear in both media psychology and data science, but be used differently.

Look For

- **Unfamiliar but recurring terms?** Consider adding them to your **master keyword list**.
- **Cited papers that don't appear in Google Scholar or PubMed?** Add them to your **citation tracker** or feed them into ResearchRabbit or Zotero for graphing.
- **Topic overlap across disciplines?** Mark this as a possible direction for interdisciplinary framing.

Example

If you searched for "TikTok" AND "mental health" and Perplexity returns a result on "short-form video content and adolescent distress," you've just uncovered a **semantic variant** and a **possibly underused search term**—"short-form video." Add it to your list.

Bonus Tip

Perplexity often shows **related questions** people ask. These can serve as prompts for refining your research question or generating sub-themes for your literature review structure.

Automate Triage and Visual Discovery

You don't need to manually read hundreds of titles and abstracts. AI tools can help you filter intelligently.

Visual Networks

- **ResearchRabbit** - Upload 3–5 promising papers. It generates a network of related work and automatically sends updates as new research appears.
- **Connected Papers** - Drop a DOI and see a concept map of the field's backbone—perfect for spotting seminal or orphan studies you might otherwise miss.

Refine, Export, and Log Transparently

Once you've run both traditional and semantic searches, combine results:

1. **Export from databases** as RIS or CSV files.
2. **Merge and deduplicate** in Zotero, EndNote, or Rayyan.
3. **Screen with AI support** (e.g., Rayyan's "predict include/exclude" feature).
4. **Version your Boolean strings**—label each variant clearly (e.g., v1, v2) and record the filters used.

To make your workflow fully transparent and reproducible, export your RIS or CSV files from each database while recording the database name, export date, total record count, and any filters used in a simple "Export Log." When you merge these files in Zotero, EndNote, or Rayyan, rely on the built-in duplicate finder but always manually verify possible matches before removing records. Prior to using AI-assisted screening features—such as Rayyan's "predict include/exclude"—write down your precise inclusion and exclusion criteria and save a copy of those settings. Finally, keep every Boolean search string under version control in a text file or Google sheets: label each variant with a version number and date, note the exact syntax and platform-specific tweaks, record the filters applied (for example, "LIMIT TO English; 2015–2025"), and briefly explain why you made each change. This detailed documentation ensures that anyone—yourself included—can retrace and audit your entire search strategy.

Day 4 Summary Box

- A well-constructed search strategy moves beyond simple keyword inputs by combining Boolean logic, database-specific syntax, and AI-enhanced tools to retrieve relevant, high-quality academic literature.
- Selection of databases should align with your research domain; platforms like PubMed, Scopus, Semantic Scholar, IEEE Xplore, and Consensus each offer strengths depending on your field.
- Advanced search techniques—such as proximity operators, field tags, truncation, and wildcards—ensure precision and help surface papers that may use alternate terminology.

- AI meta-search platforms like Consensus and Perplexity support semantic exploration, uncovering terminology drift, emerging phrases, and relevant yet undercited work

Checklist: Executing a Strategic, AI-Enhanced Literature Search

Dimension	Criteria	Check
I. Database Selection	Selected 2–3 databases aligned with the research domain (e.g., PubMed, PsycINFO, IEEE Xplore)	[ ]
	Reviewed the advanced search capabilities and syntax of each selected database	[ ]
	Included at least one AI-enhanced platform (e.g., Semantic Scholar, Consensus, Perplexity)	[ ]
II. Boolean Search Execution	Applied previously constructed Boolean string into each database	[ ]
	Used field tags to focus searches (e.g., [tiab], TITLE-ABS-KEY)	[ ]
	Included proximity operators (e.g., NEAR/3, W/3) to improve conceptual precision	[ ]
	Used truncation and wildcards to capture spelling and form variations (e.g., anxiet*, instagra*)	[ ]
III. AI Meta-Search Validation	Ran queries through Consensus or Perplexity to uncover semantically related studies	[ ]
	Identified terminology drift, alternate phrasings, or recent emerging terms	[ ]
	Added new relevant terms and sources to the master keyword list or citation tracker	[ ]
IV. Citation Network Exploration	Used ResearchRabbit or Connected Papers to explore related work via citation and concept networks	[ ]
	Added at least 3 new studies through lateral exploration of citation maps	[ ]
	Identified and noted interdisciplinary connections or novel sub-themes	[ ]
V. Results Management and Deduplication	Exported search results in standardized format (RIS, CSV, BibTeX)	[ ]
	Merged and deduplicated records using Zotero, EndNote, or Rayyan	[ ]
	Applied basic inclusion/exclusion screening using AI-assisted triage tools (e.g., Rayyan classifier)	[ ]
VI. Documentation and Transparency	Saved and versioned all Boolean strings (e.g., Search_v1, Search_v2_MeSH)	[ ]
	Recorded filters used (date range, document type, language)	[ ]
	Logged search date, tools used, and rationale for key decisions (e.g., tool choice, term inclusion)	[ ]

Day 5: AI-Powered Screening

Once your search strategy has yielded hundreds—or even thousands—of articles, the real challenge begins: **screening** and **selecting** the most relevant, high-quality sources for your literature review. This is where AI tools like **Rayyan** and **scite.ai** become invaluable. They not only accelerate the review process, but help you make smarter, evidence-informed inclusion decisions.

Rayyan: Turbocharge Your Abstract Screening

What it is:

Rayyan is a free, web-based systematic review assistant that uses machine learning to help you screen abstracts and titles rapidly—up to **90% faster** than manual screening.

How to use it:

1. **Export your search results** from databases like PubMed, Scopus, or Web of Science in .RIS, .CSV, or .BIB format.
2. **Import the file into Rayyan** and begin screening titles and abstracts by marking them as "include," "exclude," or "maybe."
3. As you tag, Rayyan's **AI model learns from your decisions** and begins prioritizing likely-relevant studies at the top of your list.
4. Use **labels, filters, and blind review features** if working with co-authors.

Why it helps:

- **Learns your inclusion logic** - The more you tag, the smarter it gets.
- **Saves mental energy** - It surfaces likely-relevant studies first, so you don't waste time on irrelevant results.
- **Supports collaboration** - You can invite collaborators to screen in parallel, with optional blinded decisions to reduce bias.

Pro Tip - Use Rayyan's "exclude reasons" feature to document why certain studies don't make the cut—great for transparency and systematic reporting later on.

scite.ai: Judge Citations by Their Scientific Strength

What it is:

Unlike traditional citation counters, adds **context** to every reference in a paper. Instead of showing just who cited a study, it tells you **how** they cited it:

- ◯ **Supporting** (positive evidence)
- ⬤ **Contrasting** (challenges or refutes)
- ◯ **Mentioning** (neutral mention)

How to use it:

1. Open a paper in **scite** or install the browser extension.
2. Hover over any citation to see how other scholars have treated it.
3. Click to read the exact sentence that supports, contrasts, or mentions the cited study.

Why it helps:

- **Prioritize stronger evidence** - Choose papers that are widely **supported**, not just frequently **mentioned**.
- **Spot controversies** - Contrasting citations flag debates in the field that may need to be acknowledged in your review.
- **Context matters** - A citation count of 300 doesn't mean much unless you know whether those 300 were praising or disputing the findings.

Pro Tip - Use scite to **validate your cornerstone studies**—those you rely on most in your argument. Ensure they're well-supported and not widely contradicted.

Integrating Both Tools into Your Workflow:

Stage	Task	Tool	Outcome
After search export	Screen for relevance	**Rayyan**	Prioritized, AI-assisted abstract screening
After reading full papers	Evaluate citation quality	**scite.ai**	Confidence in selecting studies with strong scientific backing

These tools help you **curate smarter**, not just faster. In academic writing, it's not just about quantity of sources—but the **quality and credibility** of what you include. Rayyan and scite ensure your literature review reflects both.

Capture, De-Duplicate, and Stay Synced

Once you've found valuable papers, don't let them float in a sea of browser tabs. Set up a clean, professional evidence management system:

- **Zotero + Connector**: One-click PDF saving with metadata, tags, and annotation support.

At this point, your literature search has become *alive*. You're not just searching anymore—you're subscribed to the conversation.

Once you've identified valuable papers, the real challenge is **keeping them organized**, accessible, and connected to your evolving literature review. The last thing you want is to rediscover a goldmine paper—only to realize you lost it in a sea of browser tabs or scattered PDFs. Day by day, your research library should become a curated archive that **remembers, links, and evolves** with your project.

Here's how to set up a system that works *with* your thinking, not against it.

Zotero + Browser Connector: Your Research Vault

What it is:

Zotero is a free, open-source reference manager that stores your papers, citations, and annotations in one place. With the **Zotero Connector** browser extension, you can save items from journal sites, Google Scholar, and even library databases *with a single click.*

How it works:

1. Install Zotero + Connector (Chrome/Firefox).
2. When you find a paper you want, click the browser icon—it saves the **PDF**, the **citation**, and even **tags** or journal metadata.
3. Organize into folders ("Lit Review – Social Media") and subfolders ("TikTok Studies").

Why it matters:

- Keeps **PDFs, notes, and citations** in one searchable library.
- Supports direct **citation insertion** into Word, Google Docs, and Overleaf.
- You can **annotate PDFs** or highlight key quotes right within Zotero (no more lost sticky notes).

Your Literature Library Is Now *Alive*

By this stage, you've moved from "gathering papers" to **building a living, breathing evidence ecosystem**.

You're no longer passively reading. You're **subscribed to the conversation**—curating, annotating, and evolving your understanding with every new publication.

Best Practices for a Transparent Search

The integrity of your review depends on a reproducible, auditable search strategy. Here's how to stay clean and clear:

1. **Start broad, then slice**

   Don't over-filter at the start. Run inclusive searches first, then apply filters for date, language, and type *after* export.

2. **Track hit counts**

   If adding a new term causes your results to drop drastically, check whether you introduced a rare or off-topic term.

3. **Version your search strings**

   Save them with clear names: *Instagram_Anxiety_v1.txt, ScopusQuery_v2.ris,* etc. This is especially critical for thesis appendices or systematic reviews.

Sprint Task: Your Literature Search Sprint

Set aside at least 60 minutes for today's workflow. The goal is to generate a meaningful, evidence-rich collection of articles.

Manual Tasks

1. **Search in at least two databases**
   - Paste your Boolean string into **PubMed** and **Scopus**
   - Export ≤300 results each (RIS or CSV)
2. **Skim & select 3–5 relevant papers**
   - Read titles and abstracts
   - Note relevance, novelty, and sample size or population
3. **Save articles properly**
   - Download PDFs or use Zotero Connector

AI-Enhanced Tasks

Task	Tool	Evidence
Run Boolean string	PubMed, Scopus	Save RIS/CSV files
Meta-search query	Consensus	Note any new terms added
Concept map	ResearchRabbit	Screenshot: *Day4_Graph.png*
AI screening	Rayyan	Include/exclude 20 abstracts, note accuracy
Set alerts	Litmaps / Google Scholar	Screenshot confirmation

Quick Tips & Ethical Reminders

- **Always verify AI-suggested DOIs**—hallucinations happen.
- **Record search dates and query versions**—this is essential for transparency.
- **Respect database limits**—some cap exports (e.g., Scopus = 2,000 records).

Save every RIS, CSV, screenshot, and Boolean string in an organized Day 5 folder. Trust me—your future self will thank you during writing and review.

Final Thoughts: From Searching to Curating

By now, your literature review is no longer abstract—it's tangible. You've located live evidence, skimmed real abstracts, and started to recognize voices, trends, and citation clusters in your field.

You've also taken your first big leap into AI-enhanced research workflows: structured queries, visual filters, machine-assisted screening, and continuous alerts. This is what a 2025-ready research strategy looks like.

Next, in Day 6, we'll shift gears from searching to **screening**—learning how to appraise and prioritize what you've found. Not all papers are created equal, and not every hit is worth your time. We'll apply quality filters to help you build a gold-standard review stack.

But for today, rest well—you've officially entered the literature review arena.

Sprint Task: Your Precision Refinement Workflow

Today's deliverables bring together everything you've learned in the first week of the sprint. Set aside about 70 minutes.

Manual Tasks

1. **Refine your Boolean string with proximity + field tags**
   Example: TITLE-ABS-KEY("Instagram" W/3 anxiety) AND ("college students")
2. **Apply post-export filters**
   - Date: 2018–2023
   - Document type: Peer-reviewed articles
3. **Log your query version and note improvements**
   Example: "Version 2.0 improved relevance—more focused results, less duplication"

Day 5 Summary Box

- With a refined search completed, the focus now shifts to screening—selecting the most relevant and high-quality sources from your search results using AI-enhanced tools.
- **Rayyan** streamlines abstract screening through machine learning, rapidly surfacing the most relevant studies while supporting collaborative, blinded decision-making and transparent documentation.
- **scite.ai** adds critical context to citation data by indicating whether a study is supported, contested, or merely mentioned—enabling smarter evidence selection and highlighting scholarly debates.
- Your reference management system should now be active and organized. Use **Zotero** for storage and annotation.

PART II: ORGANIZE AND EVALUATE

Day 6: From Chaos to Clarity — Building a Smart Research Library

Congratulations—you've now retrieved your first batch of relevant research articles. At this point, most graduate students make a critical mistake: they download PDFs, scatter them across desktop folders, and assume they'll remember what's what later.

You're going to do better.

Today, you'll begin building your **personal academic library**—a curated, AI-powered, metadata-rich repository that will save you hours of future frustration. It's not just about organizing files. It's about creating an **intelligent research hub** that syncs across devices, links to your notes, and evolves with every new citation or discovery.

Let's convert your document downloads into a dynamic, searchable, and auto-synced knowledge ecosystem.

Why Source Management Matters

You may not feel the pain yet—but it's coming. When you have 80+ PDFs saved across random folders, searching for "that article on Instagram and anxiety" turns into an archaeological dig. Worse, citing a study you vaguely recall but can't locate could lead to inaccuracies or even missed insights.

The solution is simple: build your system now, while your library is still small.

A well-structured research library will allow you to:

- Retrieve full texts in one click
- Rename and relocate files consistently

- Tag and categorize sources by theme, method, or population
- Annotate, summarize, and sync seamlessly to your note-taking apps
- Back everything up and share selectively

Today's chapter will show you how to do all this in under an hour.

Step 1: Capture and Auto-Retrieve PDFs with Zotero

If you haven't yet, download and install **Zotero**, the most powerful open-source reference manager for academic workflows. Then install the **Zotero Connector** browser extension.

Whenever you find a paper, simply click the connector icon. Zotero will:

- Save the full citation metadata (authors, title, journal, etc.)
- Store everything in your cloud-synced Zotero library

If no open-access version is found immediately, use Zotero's **"Find Available PDF"** option as a backup.

Step 2: Clean and Organize with ZotFile

Next, install the **ZotFile plugin**, which adds two powerful capabilities:

1. **File renaming and relocation**: Each new PDF can be automatically renamed using a format like Author_Year_Topic.pdf and saved to a custom folder, such as /Literature/To_Read.
2. **Highlight extraction**: If you annotate PDFs on a tablet, ZotFile can extract your highlights and comments into Zotero notes.

This creates clean, searchable filenames and folder structures. No more "fulltext(6).pdf" chaos.

Bonus: Use your operating system's Spotlight or search to locate files instantly by author, tag, or keyword.

Step 3: Classify with Collections, Tags, and Smart Citations

Zotero uses two main classification systems:

- **Collections**: Like folders. Use them for broader categories (e.g., "Social Media & Anxiety," "Methods – Survey Design").
- **Tags**: Like metadata. Use them for finer details (e.g., "Instagram," "College students," "GAD-7").

Structure your library with nested collections, then tag each paper with 3–5 relevant terms.

For deeper insight, install the **scite.ai plugin**. It overlays smart citation badges that show whether each study is:

- **Supporting** another study
- **Contrasting** it
- Merely **Mentioned**

This adds immediate quality signals to your reading list.

Step 4: Sync and Back Up Your Library

Zotero's cloud sync automatically backs up your metadata. To sync PDFs:

- Use **WebDAV** or link to **Google Drive** or **iCloud**
- Export a full **Better BibTeX JSON** weekly for version-controlled backup (especially useful for systematic reviews or thesis projects)

Pro tip: Save backups to a /backup/ folder in your main literature directory, and version them (e.g., Library_v1.json, Library_v2.json).

Step 5: Stay Updated with ResearchRabbit and Litmaps

Your library shouldn't be static—it should grow organically as new research appears.

- **ResearchRabbit**: Feed it your Zotero collections, and it will suggest related papers and send weekly digests based on your evolving interests.
- **Litmaps**: Generates a visual citation graph of your topic and alerts you when high-impact papers connect to your sources (20).

Together, these tools keep your research network alive and expanding—without you having to manually monitor journals or re-run searches.

Step 6: Seamless Integration with Notes and Writing

Great researchers annotate as they read. Great systems ensure those annotations don't get lost.

- **Obsidian** (for Markdown users): Use the Zotero plugin to import citation metadata, annotations, and full references into your note vault.
- **Paperpile** (for Google Docs users): Offers inline citation and PDF highlighting with cloud sync.
- **EndNote 21** (for enterprise workflows): Includes similar in-app annotation features and integrations.

With the right setup, reading a paper becomes part of your thinking and writing process—not just a passive task.

Sprint Task: Building Your Research Library (≈ 60 minutes)

By the end of today, you'll have a functioning, future-proof academic library. Here's what to do:

Manual Tasks

Step	Action	Deliverable
1	Create a local folder structure	e.g., LitReview_SocialMedia_Anxiety > To Read / Read
2	Download at least 5 full-text PDFs	Save using format like Smith2020_SocialMediaAnxiety.pdf
3	Add each to Zotero	Use the browser connector or manual import
4	Tag each with 3–5 descriptors	e.g., social media, college students, anxiety
5	Write a 1-sentence summary in Zotero's Notes field	Capture findings or sample characteristics

AI-Enhanced Tasks

Task	Tool	Outcome
Install ZotFile, scite, Better BibTeX	Zotero Plugin Pane	Screenshot of setup
Configure file naming rules in ZotFile	Zotero > Preferences > ZotFile	Screenshot of renamed file list
Enable Zotero sync + export Better BibTeX JSON	/backup/ folder	Confirmation dialog or JSON preview
Enroll your library in ResearchRabbit	Account setup + first graph	Screenshot: RR_LitGraph.png
Create Litmaps alert	Set by topic or DOI	Screenshot confirmation
Pull highlights into Obsidian (or other app)	Test with one PDF	Paste markdown snippet

Final Thoughts: You've Built the Engine

At this point in the sprint, you're no longer "collecting articles"—you're engineering an intelligent, scalable research library.

Every PDF you download is:

- Named consistently
- Indexed for easy search

- Tagged with your research themes
- Synced and backed up
- Connected to discovery and note-taking systems

You've just created a digital brain extension for your PhD. Next, in Day 7, we'll teach it to **read with purpose**.

Next up: how to triage, tag, and rapidly annotate your growing stack of papers—without drowning in detail.

Day 6 Summary Box

- A disorganized collection of PDFs can quickly derail your literature review. Today's focus is on transforming scattered documents into a searchable, intelligent academic library.
- Zotero, paired with tools like ZotFile, Unpaywall, and scite.ai, allows you to capture, organize, rename, tag, and annotate papers with consistency and clarity.
- Smart classification through **collections** and **tags** ensures every source is easily retrievable, while plugins like **scite.ai** provide immediate insight into citation quality and relevance.
- Integrations with tools such as **ResearchRabbit**, **Litmaps**, and **note-taking platforms** (e.g., Obsidian, Paperpile) create a connected, evolving research environment that supports discovery, synthesis, and writing.

Day 7: Skim with Strategy — Sorting Your Sources for Relevance

By now, your research library is well-stocked and intelligently organized. You've harvested dozens of potentially useful articles, built a high-functioning Zotero setup, and established a pipeline for continual updates.

But now comes the critical filter: **Which papers actually deserve your time and attention?**

Welcome to Day 7—the day we don't read everything.

Contrary to what many graduate students assume, reading every paper cover to cover is not only inefficient, it's counterproductive. Today's task is to skim your literature stack smartly—supported by AI tools—to sort your sources into clear tiers of relevance. This triage will help you focus on what matters and discard what doesn't.

Why Skimming Is Strategic (Not Lazy)

Effective researchers don't read more—they read better.

Skimming helps you:

- Avoid time wasted on off-topic or low-quality papers
- Identify high-value sources for deeper review
- Spot patterns in findings, terminology, and methods
- Build a map of your research landscape faster

You're not ignoring nuance—you're **staging your reading**. And now, with AI assistance, you can skim smarter than ever before.

Step 1: Skim ≠ Speed Read — Use Layers

Start with the **Title and Abstract**. Ask:

- Does this directly relate to my research question?
- What is the study population?
- What kind of outcome or variables are being measured?

If promising, move to the **Introduction** and **Conclusion**. These sections often outline the rationale, aim, and key findings.

Next, scan the **Methods** and **Results**. Look for:

- Sample size
- Instruments used (e.g., anxiety scales)
- Type of analysis (e.g., regression, thematic coding)
- Effect size or significance level

Tip: Use **Ctrl+F** (or Cmd+F) to search for keywords like "Instagram," "anxiety," "college," or "survey" in the full text.

You can now rate the paper's relevance—without reading every line.

Step 2: Add the AI Triage Layer

Here's where your AI toolkit accelerates the process:

Stage	Human Step	AI Shortcut	Tool
Abstract & Title	Check fit with your question	One-line summary	Semantic Scholar TLDR
Intro & Conclusion	Read key sections	Key claims extracted	Elicit "Summarize PDF"
Methods / Results	Scan for variables/stats	Sample & limitations flash cards	Scholarcy
Credibility	Judge evidence strength	Support/contrast badges	scite.ai
Relevance Score	Sort into tiers	Smart predictions	Rayyan

Use these tools to reduce friction: they surface core content, flag weaknesses, and allow you to spend less time on irrelevant PDFs.

Step 3: Classify: High, Medium, or Low Relevance

After you skim and AI-check each paper, label it:

- **High**: Directly answers your research question or supports your framework
- **Medium**: Related but tangential (e.g., different population, adjacent concept)
- **Low**: Background or off-topic

Apply these tags in **Zotero** using the tag pane, or move items into relevance-based **collections**.

Example:

- *Smith (2020)* — High: Instagram use and anxiety among undergraduates
- *Johnson (2019)* — Medium: Social media and depression in adults
- *Chen (2018)* — Low: Examines mental health apps, not platforms

Step 4: Document the Essentials

In your Zotero notes (or wherever you centralize insights), record:

- A **1-sentence summary** of the main finding
- The **sample** (e.g., "N = 300 college students")
- Any **notable limitations**
- Your personal **judgment** on why it matters

If using **Scholarcy** or **Elicit**, you can paste key bullets directly into the notes field.

This becomes the foundation of your **literature matrix** (coming on Day 8)—an essential tool for synthesis.

Step 5: Sync to Note-Taking Tools

For "High" relevance papers, pull your summaries into **Obsidian**, **Notion**, or **Roam** using Zotero plugins. This ensures your deep-dive notes are aligned with your knowledge base.

This way, your ideas aren't trapped in PDFs—they live where your writing does.

Sprint Task: Skim, Tag, and Summarize (≈ 45 min)

This practical session ensures your library is prioritized and primed for synthesis.

Task	Tool	Deliverable
Skim 5 PDFs	Human + AI	Rate as High / Medium / Low
Use Scholarcy / Elicit	Generate summaries	Paste 5 summaries into Zotero notes
Quality Check	scite.ai	Record support vs. contrast count
Label in Zotero	Tag by relevance	Screenshot of tag pane
Sync into Obsidian	One "High" note + highlights	Paste a snippet from your markdown

Sample Walkthrough:

- *Smith2020_SocialMediaAnxiety.pdf*

  Scholarcy Summary: Sample size 300 undergrads; measured Instagram time and GAD-7; positive correlation.
  scite: 7 supporting citations, 0 contrasting.
  Tag: High Relevance
  Note: "Instagram >3h correlates w/ ↑ anxiety; sample = U.S. college students; cross-sectional; no gender control."

Quick Reference: AI Prompts

Elicit
"Summarize the key findings, sample size, and limitations of this PDF."
Scholarcy
"Generate a 5-bullet flash card summary and highlight any limitations."
ChatGPT
"Rate the likely relevance of this abstract to 'Instagram use & anxiety in college students' as High / Medium / Low and justify."

Common Pitfalls and How to Avoid Them

- **Trusting AI blindly**

  Always double-check key figures like sample size and effect size. AI tools hallucinate occasionally.

- **Skipping figures and tables**

  Visuals often hold more insight than abstracts. Don't rely on text alone.

- **Confirmation bias**

  scite's "contrasting" badge helps you find papers that challenge your assumptions—don't ignore them.

Final Thoughts: Build the Signal, Reduce the Noise

Your goal today wasn't to absorb everything—it was to sort wisely. You now have:

- A relevance-ranked literature queue
- Smart notes and summaries inside your library
- A trimmed-down, high-value subset of papers

You've turned a chaotic PDF dump into a structured reading workflow. Every paper in your "High" set now deserves deeper reading and annotation—coming next in **Day 8** on synthesis and thematic coding.

This is how scholars prepare to write: not with overwhelmed minds, but with organized knowledge.

Day 7 Summary Box

- Reading every paper in full is inefficient and often unnecessary. Strategic skimming—guided by your research question and AI support—enables faster, more accurate filtering of relevant literature.
- Skim in layers: title, abstract, introduction, conclusion, and, when needed, methods/results. Use keyword search (e.g., Ctrl+F) to locate critical concepts quickly.
- AI tools such as **Scholarcy**, **Elicit**, **Semantic Scholar TLDR**, and **scite.ai** help extract summaries, highlight limitations, and surface evidence strength—accelerating triage without sacrificing rigor.
- Classify each paper as **High**, **Medium**, or **Low** relevance, and label/tag them in your reference manager accordingly. Document essential metadata and insights for future synthesis.

Day 8: From Reading to Reasoning — Taking Smart Notes for Synthesis

Reading and tagging papers is important—but it's what you *do* with those papers that turns scattered knowledge into a solid literature review.

Today marks a pivotal transition in your 30-day sprint: you'll move from scanning PDFs to extracting insights, paraphrasing findings, and encoding your knowledge into structured, searchable notes. In short, you'll build a personal *evidence base*—ready to fuel paragraph-level writing and thematic synthesis in the coming days.

We're not talking about copy-pasting highlights. We're talking about building a high-integrity, AI-assisted **literature matrix**—a synthesis-ready record of each study's key facts, relevance, quality, and implications.

Let's turn reading into retention.

Why Structured Notes Matter

Taking effective notes isn't just a memory aid—it's a strategic thinking process.

Studies show that **paraphrased summaries** significantly improve comprehension and long-term recall. Unlike copying and pasting, paraphrasing activates higher-order cognitive functions: comparison, interpretation, and synthesis. It also prevents accidental plagiarism down the line.

A structured literature matrix, whether in a spreadsheet, Notion board, or Markdown vault, allows you to:

- **Compare methods and findings** across studies
- **Tag gaps and limitations** for discussion
- **Filter by themes, populations, and relevance**
- **Build arguments paragraph by paragraph**

So let's begin by moving three of your "High Relevance" papers into structured, summarized form.

Step 1: Extract Key Facts in Seconds Using AI

Rather than manually combing through PDFs, start with **AI-powered summarizers** to gather key elements.

Tool	Pulls Out	How to Use
Scholarcy	Study aim, methods, sample, key results, limitations	Drag & drop PDF; copy "flash card" bullets into Zotero
Elicit	Design, PICO elements, outcome metrics, headline findings	Paste in title/DOI or upload PDF
Semantic Scholar	One-sentence summaries for rapid triage	Hover over "TLDR" to get quick overview

You now have structured highlights. But don't stop there.

Step 2: Paraphrase and Add Reflection

This step is critical.

Take each AI-generated bullet and **rephrase it in your own words**. Then add a **commentary line** that connects the finding to your topic.

Example
Scholarcy: "Survey of 200 U.S. undergraduates; students using Instagram >3 hrs/day had significantly higher GAD-7 scores." **Paraphrased**: Smith (2020) surveyed 200 college students and found those using Instagram over three hours daily scored higher on anxiety scales.

Reflection: This supports my hypothesis but lacks control for gender or academic pressure.

Store these in your **Zotero Notes**, or in **Obsidian's front matter** if you're working in Markdown. These paraphrased notes are what you'll *quote, reference,* and *synthesize* later.

Step 3: Encode into a Literature Matrix

Now build your **literature matrix**—your structured database of key papers.

Use Excel, Google Sheets, Notion, or Obsidian tables. At a minimum, include:

Column	Description
Citation	Author, Year, Title
Purpose	What was the study trying to do?
Method	Survey, experiment, meta-analysis, etc.
Population	Sample characteristics
Key Findings	Main outcomes and effect sizes
Limitations	As noted by authors or you
Relevance	High / Medium / Low
Quality Signal	scite.ai: # supporting / # contrasting

You'll populate this matrix as you go—and in the next chapter, it becomes the foundation for thematic coding and structured argumentation.

Step 4: Sync for Retrieval and Reuse

Now connect your note ecosystem:

- **Zotero → Obsidian**
  Use the Zotero Markdown plugin to sync your metadata, paraphrased notes, and highlights into standalone literature notes.
- **Notion Integration**
  If you prefer a cloud-first interface, Notion tables or kanban boards can replicate your literature matrix and allow tagging and filtering.
- **ResearchRabbit Learning Loop**
  Once a paper is tagged "High Relevance," add it to your ResearchRabbit collection. The system will push closely related papers to your digest weekly—adding to your matrix without manual searching.

Pro Tips and Pitfalls to Avoid

Do This	✕ Avoid This	Why
Use your own words	Don't paste AI text verbatim	Enhances understanding, avoids plagiarism
Tag limitations explicitly	Don't ignore study weaknesses	Helps later during critical appraisal
Cross-check numbers	Don't trust AI blindly	Tables often misread by NLP tools
Use quote blocks sparingly	Don't over-rely on direct quotes	Quotes are for powerful phrasing or exact stats only

Pro tip: If a quote is essential, add the **page number** and context to your note immediately.

Sprint Task: Synthesis-Ready Notes (≈ 60 min)

This hands-on work converts your best papers into structured, retrievable insight blocks.

Task	Tool	Deliverable
1. Extract & Paraphrase **3 papers**	Scholarcy or Elicit + Zotero	Zotero note with both original + paraphrased bullet points
2. Matrix Entry	Walden University Excel template / Notion DB	Populate 3 rows with full fields
3. Quality Check	scite.ai	Add column for # of supporting vs. contrasting citations
4. Sync	Zotero + Obsidian or Notion	Screenshot of synced note
5. Reflect	Journal or note field	Write 100-word reflection on how paraphrasing changed your understanding

Sample Matrix Entry (Smith, 202

Citation	Purpose	Method	Key Finding	Limitation	Relevance	Quality
Smith (2020)	To assess Instagram use and anxiety	Survey, N = 200 undergrads	>3hr/day users had 20% ↑ GAD-7 scores	No gender control; cross-sectional	High	7 supporting / 0 contrasting

Final Thoughts: You're Now Building Evidence, Not Just Notes

At this point, you've transformed passive reading into active reasoning. You're no longer drowning in PDFs—you're **organizing arguments, insights, and limitations** in a format that feeds directly into writing.

Next, in Day 9, you'll begin coding these entries—grouping them into thematic buckets and linking them to your research framework. This is where synthesis begins, and where literature stops being background and starts becoming your argument.

Day 8 Summary Box

- Effective literature reviews begin with structured, paraphrased notes—not passive highlights. Today's focus is on extracting, rephrasing, and recording core insights from your highest-priority papers.
- AI tools such as **Scholarcy**, **Elicit**, and **Semantic Scholar** streamline initial extraction, but manual paraphrasing and reflection are essential for comprehension, originality, and synthesis.
- A structured **literature matrix** captures key details: purpose, method, population, findings, limitations, relevance, and quality—serving as the foundation for coding and argumentation.
- Integrating your notes into platforms like **Zotero**, **Obsidian**, or **Notion** ensures your insights are searchable, retrievable, and connected to your broader thinking.

Day 9: From Notes to Narratives — Discovering Themes and Patterns

You've read the papers. You've taken structured, paraphrased notes. Now, it's time to step back and look at the bigger picture.

Day 9 is about **synthesis**—the heart of the literature review.

You're no longer a collector of citations. You're now a storyteller, identifying recurring themes, mapping contradictions, and surfacing intellectual patterns that will form the backbone of your literature review structure.

While traditional thematic sorting required color-coded index cards or sticky-note walls, today you'll use a suite of AI-powered and visual tools to accelerate and clarify your thematic thinking. This chapter guides you through a structured process to identify, cluster, and document 3–5 major themes that connect your literature into a coherent scholarly narrative.

Why Thematic Discovery Matters

Your literature review isn't a list of summaries—it's a conceptual map of your research domain.

Identifying themes:

- Helps you avoid "narrative sprawl" (a PRISMA trap)
- Clarifies where your research fits in or diverges
- Provides a blueprint for your chapter outline
- Reveals areas of consensus, contention, and neglect

Without thematic structure, your review risks becoming descriptive. With it, you produce synthesis—and signal academic mastery.

Step 1: Export and Prepare Your Bibliographic Data

Before diving into visualization or coding, prepare your library data.

- In **Zotero**, select your High and Medium relevance collections (≥ 30 papers).
- Export as .RIS or .BibTeX.
- Clean up duplicates using Zotero's "Duplicate Items" view.

This clean dataset is what you'll feed into bibliometric mapping tools.

Save the file as: Day9_LibraryExport.ris

Step 2: Use AI and Mapping Tools to Suggest Themes

Here's where machine learning meets scholarly instinct.

Co-occurrence Clustering — *VOSviewer*

Upload your .RIS file to **VOSviewer** (21). It generates a keyword heatmap, showing how concepts cluster across your library. Focus on 3–7 prominent clusters.

Example:
Cluster A: "Instagram," "screen time," "usage frequency"
Cluster B: "anxiety," "mental health," "depression"
Cluster C: "peer comparison," "self-esteem," "body image"

Citation Graphing — *Connected Papers* or *Litmaps*

Paste a central DOI from each cluster into **Connected Papers** or **Litmaps**. These tools visualize thematic "families" based on citation similarity. Watch for:

- **Central hubs** → Seminal works
- **Peripheral nodes** → Niche or underexplored areas

Save your map and annotate surprising outliers or topic gaps.

Semantic Bridging — *InfraNodus (Optional)*

Paste 4–5 abstracts into **InfraNodus** (22). It builds a network graph of concepts, highlighting "bridging terms" (e.g., *self-esteem, peer comparison*) that connect otherwise distinct themes.

These bridges often reveal novel research angles or unexplored intersections.

Step 3: Cross-Validate Themes with Qualitative Tools

Now test whether your AI-suggested clusters match your human-coded notes.

Auto Theme Coding — *NVivo 14 or ATLAS.ti AI*

Upload your five most relevant PDFs to **NVivo**. Use the Auto-Coding function to identify key themes, sentiments, and co-occurrence patterns.

Then, compare:

- Which NVivo themes match your **VOSviewer clusters**?
- Where do **qualitative codes** diverge or refine bibliometric categories?

Add **scite.ai citation badges** to see whether each theme includes **supporting**, **contrasting**, or **mixed-evidence** papers.

Step 4: Build a Codebook of Themes

You now have the material to draft a **Theme Codebook**—your synthesis blueprint.

Theme	Definition	Representative Papers	Consensus	Key Gaps
Social Media Usage Time	Frequency/duration of platform use	Smith (2020), Lee (2021)	Mostly supporting	Few studies distinguish passive vs. active use
Comparison & Self-Esteem	Peer comparison effects on mental health	Kim (2019), Patel (2022)	Mixed results	Lacks cross-cultural studies
Demographics	Age/gender as moderators of impact	Chen (2021), Morales (2020)	Consensus: women report higher anxiety	Few longitudinal studies

Then tag your Zotero entries accordingly:

theme::usage_time, theme::peer_comparison, theme::demographics

Use **Obsidian Dataview** to auto-rollup notes tagged by theme—creating dynamic dashboards that will evolve with your review.

Common Pitfalls and How to Avoid Them

Pitfall	Solution
Overreliance on frequent terms	Rare concepts may matter more—cross-check with manual notes
Too many or too few themes	Aim for **3–5 themes** to balance nuance and narrative coherence
Missing dissent	Use **scite.ai's contrasting badge** to flag internal contradictions

Also: remember that clusters are **cues**, not conclusions. Let AI guide your attention—but your judgment must still decide.

Sprint Task: Build Your Thematic Map (≈ 70 min)

Today's outputs are foundational. By completing them, you'll produce a robust thematic architecture for structuring your literature review chapters.

Task	Tool	Deliverable
Export RIS file & run VOSviewer	Zotero + VOSviewer	Screenshot: Day9_VOS.png with 3+ clusters
Run Litmaps on 3 seed DOIs	Litmaps	Map image Day9_Litmap.png + 100-word note
Paste abstracts into InfraNodus	InfraNodus	Exported PDF: Day9_Infra.pdf
Auto-code 5 PDFs in NVivo	NVivo 14	Comparison table: AI themes vs. clusters
Build 3–5-theme Codebook	Spreadsheet / Notion	Include "Key Gap" column
Tag Zotero items & test Dataview	Zotero + Obsidian	Screenshot of live theme table

Final Thoughts: You're Building the Framework for Argument

By the end of today, you've achieved what most students only reach at the final writing stage: a clear **narrative logic**. Your literature is no longer a pile of isolated studies—it's a structured ecosystem of **themes, patterns, and gaps**.

From here on, you'll write not by summarizing individual papers, but by advancing arguments within each theme, contrasting evidence, and highlighting your contribution.

Next, in Day 10, we'll go even further: we'll visualize this structure as a **conceptual map**—a lit review body outline you can literally see.

Day 9 Summary Box

- Today marks the shift from collecting insights to synthesizing them. The goal is to identify and cluster 3–5 key themes that form the conceptual backbone of your literature review.
- Tools like **VOSviewer**, **Connected Papers**, **InfraNodus**, and **NVivo** help visualize co-occurring terms, citation networks, and thematic bridges—accelerating theme discovery across your curated sources.
- Your **Theme Codebook** should include theme definitions, representative studies, level of consensus, and identified research gaps—providing a clear outline for your review structure.
- Cross-validation of themes using both AI-assisted clustering and qualitative coding ensures your synthesis is robust, balanced, and grounded in both patterns and anomalies.

Checklist: Discovering Themes and Building Your Literature Framework

Dimension	Criteria	Check
I. Library Preparation	Exported High/Medium relevance papers from Zotero as .RIS or .BibTeX format	[ ]
	Removed duplicates using Zotero's "Duplicate Items" feature	[ ]
	Saved export file clearly (e.g., Day9_LibraryExport.ris)	[ ]
II. Bibliometric Theme Discovery	Uploaded .RIS file to **VOSviewer** and identified at least 3–5 clusters	[ ]
	Interpreted clusters by keyword grouping and saved heatmap screenshot	[ ]
	Explored citation families using **Connected Papers** or **Litmaps**	[ ]
	Annotated central hubs, peripheral nodes, and unexpected outliers	[ ]
	Used **InfraNodus** to extract bridging terms and thematic overlaps across 4–5 abstracts	[ ]
III. Qualitative Theme Validation	Selected 5 high-relevance PDFs and uploaded to **NVivo 14** or **ATLAS.ti**	[ ]
	Used auto-coding to extract qualitative themes, categories, or sentiment clusters	[ ]
	Compared NVivo/AI-generated themes with VOSviewer and InfraNodus results	[ ]
	Used **scite.ai** to assess levels of consensus/contrast within each major theme	[ ]
IV. Thematic Codebook Development	Created 3–5 theme categories with working definitions	[ ]
	Added representative papers, summary of consensus, and noted key research gaps for each theme	[ ]
	Recorded codebook in structured format (e.g., Notion DB, Excel, or Markdown table)	[ ]
V. System Integration and Tagging	Tagged each relevant Zotero entry with its corresponding theme (theme::name)	[ ]
	Verified that theme tags allow for filtering and search functionality in Zotero or Obsidian	[ ]
	Tested Dataview or Kanban plugins (if using Obsidian or Notion) to auto-group notes by theme	[ ]
VI. Documentation and Archiving	Saved screenshots of VOSviewer, Litmaps, and InfraNodus visualizations	[ ]
	Exported updated Zotero collection or Better BibTeX file for backup (Day9_ThematicLibrary.json)	[ ]
	Wrote a 100-word reflection summarizing how today's work reshaped your understanding of the topic	[ ]

Day 10: Seeing the Story — Visualizing Connections with Concept Maps and Matrices

You've mined the literature. You've coded for themes. Now it's time to step back, widen your lens, and **see the field as a whole**.

On Day 10, we shift from textual analysis to visual synthesis. You'll use tools like concept maps, bibliometric graphs, and literature matrices to construct a panoramic, structured view of your research domain—one that reveals both what's known and what's missing.

Why? Because when it comes time to write, you won't just recall facts. You'll **see the architecture of your argument**—and that clarity can only come from mapping the terrain.

Why Visual Mapping Matters

Your brain processes structure faster than it processes sentences. By externalizing your research themes in diagrams or tables, you:

- **Condense complexity** into clear relationships
- **Spot missing variables** or underexplored populations
- **Clarify how your research fits** into the scholarly conversation
- **Build an outline-ready scaffold** for chapter writing

Whether you're a visual thinker or not, this phase transforms your knowledge from abstract to navigable.

Step 1: Export Clean Data from Zotero

Begin by preparing your data for visual processing:

1. In **Zotero**, select your High and Medium relevance items.
2. Click **File** ⍰ **Export** and choose **RIS** format.
3. De-duplicate items before export to avoid double nodes in maps.

Save your export file as:

Day10_LibraryExport.ris

This file powers your bibliometric and citation maps.

Step 2: Generate a Bibliometric Map (VOSviewer or Litmaps)

Use VOSviewer for Keyword Clustering

- Open VOSviewer → Create Map → Choose *Co-occurrence* → *All keywords*
- Set a minimum occurrence threshold (e.g., 3–5)
- The tool generates color-coded clusters representing natural topic groupings

Example:

- Cluster A: "Instagram," "usage," "screen time"
- Cluster B: "anxiety," "depression," "mental health"
- Cluster C: "self-esteem," "peer comparison," "body image"

Use Connected Papers or Litmaps for Citation Networks

- Paste a representative DOI from each VOSviewer cluster
- Explore:
    - *Prior Works* → Foundational studies
    - *Derivations* → Emerging directions
- Identify isolated nodes (papers no one cites or builds on)—possible gaps

Save and label screenshots from both tools for reference.

Step 3: Overlay Your Own Concept Map

Bibliometric maps show structure. Your concept map shows **meaning**.

Using **XMind**, **draw.io**, or pen and paper:

- Place your **research question** in the center (e.g., *Social Media & Anxiety*)
- Create branches for your 3–5 major **themes**
- Under each theme, list key **papers** (Author, Year) and **findings**
- Use:
    - → **Solid arrows** for supporting findings
    - → **Dashed arrows** for contradictory results (from scite.ai)
- Color-code:
    - ◯ Green = strong consensus
    - ◯ Yellow = mixed evidence
    - ● Red = weak/inconclusive

This map becomes your "storyboard" for paragraph-level synthesis.

Step 4: Build a Structured Literature Matrix

This matrix lets you compare papers systematically.

Study	Usage Time	Content Type	Demographics	Outcome Measure	Notes
Smith 2020	↑ anxiety >3h/day	–	Undergrads	GAD-7	Small sample
Lee 2021	↑ stress >1.8h FB	Passive scrolling ↑	First-year	PSS-10	Survey-based
Chen 2019	No effect of content	Negative news ↑ anxiety	Adults (25–40)	BAI	Mixed results

Steps:

- Use the paraphrased bullets from **Day 8**
- Populate cells with short summaries

- Highlight **empty cells in red** to flag underexplored areas

This matrix can evolve as you synthesize deeper or uncover new studies.

Step 5: Use InfraNodus to Find Bridging Concepts (Optional)

Bridging terms connect different clusters—often revealing underexplored angles.

Steps:

1. Paste 10–15 abstracts into **InfraNodus**
2. View the semantic network
3. Identify nodes with **high betweenness centrality**
   - These often represent **bridging ideas** (e.g., *self-esteem, moderation, platform type*)
4. Jot a hypothesis:

> "Self-esteem appears as a link between social comparison and anxiety. Few studies isolate it—may be worth exploring."

Export the concept graph PDF for your visuals folder.

Step 6: Store, Version, and Link Visuals

Organize your files:

- Create folder: /visuals/v1/
- Save:
  - Day10_VOS.png
  - Day10_ConceptMap.png
  - Day10_LitMatrix.xlsx
  - Day10_InfraGraph.pdf

In **Obsidian**, create a note titled 00_Lit_Visuals and use #viz tag. Embed image previews so they're accessible while writing.

Dataview can auto-pull visuals tagged by theme or project.

Common Pitfalls and How to Avoid Them

Pitfall	Fix
Overinterpreting rare clusters	Verify sample sizes and research design before elevating them to full themes
Color bias in visual maps	Add explicit labels and legends to avoid misreading significance
Static thinking	Schedule a refresh every 4 weeks—tools like Litmaps offer alerts for new studies in each cluster

Sprint Task: Visual Synthesis (≈ 70 min)

Task	Tool	Deliverable
1. Create VOSviewer keyword map	Zotero → RIS → VOSviewer	Screenshot Day10_VOS.png
2. Build a 2-level concept map	XMind or draw.io	PNG: Day10_ConceptMap.png
3. Fill a literature matrix	Spreadsheet / Notion	Matrix with ≥10 studies, 5 columns
4. Run InfraNodus	InfraNodus	PDF graph + 1 bridging hypothesis
5. Link visuals in Obsidian	Obsidian note + #viz tag	Screenshot of 00_Lit_Visuals note

Final Thoughts: From Clusters to Chapters

You now hold a **bird's-eye view** of the research landscape—a visual GPS for your next phase. This map is more than aesthetic. It guides:

- How you structure your literature review body
- Which themes deserve paragraph-level focus
- Where your research can fill a gap

Next, in Day 11, we'll take this visual clarity and begin mapping it into your **chapter structure**, outlining how each theme will unfold, and how your review will build momentum toward your research question.

With your research question refined, your sources screened, and your conceptual landscape visually mapped, you're now standing on solid ground. What once felt like a mountain of disconnected articles has been organized into clear themes, visual frameworks, and annotated insights. In the next phase of your sprint, you'll begin transforming that structure into scholarly prose. Starting next, we'll move from mapping the literature to writing it—section by section—beginning with a strong, strategic introduction. You're no longer gathering information; you're building your argument.

Day 10 Summary Box

- Today's focus is on transforming your structured notes and themes into visual frameworks that reveal the intellectual structure of your research domain.
- Bibliometric tools like **VOSviewer**, **Connected Papers**, and **InfraNodus** help uncover clusters, bridging terms, and citation gaps across your literature library.
- Concept mapping and literature matrices translate your findings into visual narratives—clarifying how studies connect, where evidence converges or conflicts, and which gaps remain.
- Visual tools enable you to spot patterns, surface underexplored variables, and prepare your review for paragraph-level synthesis and argumentation.

PART III: WRITE THE REVIEW

Day 11: Audit and Advance — Evaluating Sources and Spotting Gaps

You've collected. You've coded. You've clustered. Now it's time to **curate**—to critically evaluate your sources for credibility, recency, and methodological rigor, and to surface the **evidence gaps** that your literature review (and future study) will help fill.

On Day 11, we move from inclusion to discernment. You'll identify what stays, what goes, and what's missing—not through intuition alone, but through an AI-assisted, checklist-based appraisal process.

This step transforms a descriptive review into an evaluative, argument-driven synthesis—one grounded in **high-quality evidence** and a clearly defined **research contribution**.

Why Appraisal and Gap Detection Matter

Not all citations are created equal. If you want to write a strong, defensible literature review, you must:

- Weed out outdated or low-rigor studies
- Weight findings based on methodological strength
- Identify missing perspectives, populations, or variables
- Justify your own research as a logical next step

This isn't optional. It's what separates a **summary of research** from a **critical synthesis**—and it positions you as a credible contributor to the scholarly conversation.

Step 1: Appraise Each Source Using Established Checklists

Different types of studies require different evaluation lenses. Use the **JBI (Joanna Briggs Institute) checklists**, a global standard for evidence appraisal.

Study Type	Checklist
Randomized Trials	JBI RCT Checklist
Non-Randomized	JBI Quasi-Experimental Checklist
Systematic Reviews	JBI SR Checklist
Qualitative Studies	JBI Qual Checklist

Each checklist includes ~10 items (e.g., Was the sample clearly defined? Were outcomes measured reliably?). Score each **Yes = 1, No = 0**, then total the raw quality score.

Use an Excel sheet or JBI's online templates to streamline scoring.

Step 2: Enhance Scoring with Smart Citation Signals

Install the **scite.ai browser plug-in** or Zotero add-on. This overlays citation badges onto each article:

- ◯ **Supporting** → Cited by studies agreeing with its findings
- ⬤ **Mentioning** → Neutral citation
- ⬤ **Contrasting** → Cited by studies that disagree

Adjust your quality score downward by 1 point if a paper has more contrasting than supporting citations—or if it's been retracted.

Example:
Smith (2020): JBI Score = 9/10
scite = 3 supporting, 0 contrasting → ◯ Confirm
Lee (2021): JBI Score = 8/10
scite = 2 contrasting, 1 supporting → ⚠ Flag for caution

Step 3: Visualize Coverage and Detect Gaps

VOSviewer Overlay by Year

- Reload your RIS file into **VOSviewer**
- Select **Overlay Visualization** > Year of Publication
- Studies will now be color-coded by date

If a thematic cluster skews older than 2018, it may be **outdated**. Flag it.

Topical Gaps with Litmaps & ResearchRabbit

- Use **Litmaps Monitor** to track themes with no recent additions
- In **ResearchRabbit**, if a key theme (e.g., TikTok anxiety) returns **no "related" papers**, that's a structural gap

Confirm with OpenAlex

Run a **vector search** in **OpenAlex** using queries like:

```
"TikTok" AND "anxiety" AND "undergraduates"
```

If **no results** are returned (and alternate phrasings fail too), you've likely found a **legitimate research gap**.

Save screenshots of these "zero result" searches as part of your documentation trail.

Step 4: Quantify Themes in Qualitative Tools

If you've auto-coded PDFs in **NVivo 14**:

- Run the **Node Frequency Report**
- Nodes (themes) with **< 3 coded sources** indicate underdeveloped areas

Example:
theme::self_comparison → 8 papers
theme::platform_design → 1 paper → ⚠ Explore further or frame as a gap

Step 5: Write Evidence-Backed Gap Statements

Now you can draft short, powerful **gap statements** using this formula:

[Gap] + [Evidence] + [Why it matters]

Gap	Evidence	Why it Matters
No research on TikTok and anxiety among teens	0 results in OpenAlex, Litmaps Monitor silent	TikTok is the most-used app among adolescents globally
90% of studies focus on U.S./Europe	VOSviewer country metadata shows Western dominance	Limits generalizability to Middle East & Asia

Store these gap statements in a file titled:

gap_statements.md

Add tags like #justification, #originality, or #intro-material.

Sprint Task: Evidence Appraisal and Gap Detection (≈ 60 min)

Task	Tool	Deliverable
Appraise 10 studies using JBI checklist	JBI / Excel	Update literature matrix with scores
Install and apply scite plug-in	scite.ai	Record support/contrast counts in Zotero
Run VOSviewer overlay visualization	VOSviewer	Screenshot clusters <2018
Search for gaps in OpenAlex	OpenAlex	Screenshot "0 results" query
Write 2 gap statements	Obsidian or Markdown	Save as gap_statements.md

Common Pitfalls and How to Avoid Them

Pitfall	Fix
Over-reliance on one criterion	Use combined score: JBI + scite
Assuming "no hits" = a gap	Try synonyms and alternative phrasings
Ignoring recent but unreplicated studies	Flag for "emerging" status, not full consensus

Pro Tip: If a study scores below 70% or is mostly contrasted in scite, relegate it to "background" rather than "core evidence."

Final Thoughts: Lean, Clean, and Purpose-Driven

By the end of today, you've transformed your literature base from a thematic collection into a **quality-controlled, strategically filtered body of evidence**.

You now know:

- Which studies are trustworthy
- Which gaps justify your contribution
- Which themes need reinforcement

Next, in Day 12, you'll use this clarity to outline your **literature review argument**—theme by theme, point by point, with every claim backed by defensible evidence.

Day 11 Summary Box

- Today's focus is on critically appraising your sources for quality, recency, and credibility using structured checklists (e.g., JBI) and citation analysis tools like **scite.ai**.
- A dual scoring approach—combining JBI quality checklists with smart citation badges—helps you determine which studies to prioritize, flag, or exclude.
- Bibliometric overlays (e.g., publication year in **VOSviewer**) and semantic tools (e.g., **OpenAlex**, **Litmaps**) help surface topical and temporal gaps in the literature.
- Underdeveloped themes, outdated clusters, and missing population perspectives form the basis for concise, evidence-backed **research gap statements**.

Day 12: Building the Blueprint — Creating a Structured Outline

The best writing starts with smart structure. On Day 12, you stop gathering and start organizing. You'll transform your thematic map and gap analysis into a **draftable outline** for your literature review chapter—turning research clutter into logical flow.

You won't write the full chapter yet. But by the end of today, you'll have:

- The right structure for your field
- Thematic headings that flow from context to contribution
- Evidence placed strategically under each section
- A clear landing spot for your gap and rationale

This is where your reading becomes argument.

Why a Structured Outline Matters

A literature review is more than a series of summaries—it's an argument scaffold.

Outlining helps you:

- Establish a logical sequence (from broad context to specific gaps)
- Avoid overdeveloping minor themes or skipping important ones
- Reserve dedicated space for your research justification
- Draft with direction instead of discovery-mode meandering

Research from SAGE, Monash, and Purdue confirms that outlines using a **funnel-shaped structure** or **parallel thematic headings** lead to clearer, more persuasive chapters.

Choosing the Right Outline Model

Your topic, field, and audience influence how you should structure your chapter. Use the guide below:

Model	When to Use	Sections Example
Funnel (Broad→Narrow)	Topics with an established background	Introduction → Context → Latest Evidence → Gaps → Conclusion
Thematic	Interdisciplinary, emerging fields	Introduction → Theme A → Theme B → Gaps → Conclusion
Methodological	Focus on comparing study designs	Intro → Quantitative → Qualitative → Gaps → Conclusion
Chronological	Emphasizing historical development	Intro → 2000–2005 → 2006–2013 → Gaps → Conclusion

Recommendation - Use a **Funnel–Thematic hybrid**: overall chapter funnels toward the gap, while body sections follow themes internally.

Step-by-Step: Creating Your Outline

Step 1: Draft Section Headings

Use your themes from **Day 9** and structure them from broad → specific. Begin each heading with a **parallel noun or verb-turned-noun phrase** (e.g., *Social Media Usage Patterns, Effects on Anxiety, Moderating Factors*).

Example Headings:

I. Introduction
II. Patterns of Social Media Use
III. Psychological Outcomes: Anxiety and Stress
IV. Moderating Factors (e.g., Content, Demographics)
V. Gaps and Study Rationale
VI. Conclusion

Ensure parallel structure. If one heading starts with a noun, they all should.

Step 2: Populate Each Section with Bullets

Under each heading, add:

- **Key findings** (use short citation placeholders like *Smith 2020*)
- **Contrasts or contradictions** if applicable
- **Your synthesis notes** from Day 8

Example - Section III:

III. Psychological Outcomes: Anxiety and Stress

- Smith (2020): Instagram >3hr/day → ↑ anxiety in undergraduates
- Lee (2021): Passive scrolling linked to stress (Facebook)
- Contrasting result: Chen (2019) - no significant effect from daily use

Use Zotero's **Better BibTeX plugin** to export citations directly into Markdown or Notion if you're working digitally.

Step 3: Insert Gap Statement at the Right Moment

Reserve a dedicated section—just before your conclusion—for articulating the research gap.

Pull your strongest gap statement from Day 11 and place it here, supported by matrix data.

V. Gaps and Study Rationale

- "Few studies explore the mental health impact of TikTok use among non-Western students."
- Litmaps monitor + OpenAlex query = 0 relevant results
- This gap informs the rationale for the current study

This creates a clear **handoff to your research**—critical for coherence and justification.

Step 4: Apply Quality Control

Use the following checklist:

Quality Element	Check
Headings are parallel	☑
Logical flow (broad → specific → gap)	☑
At least 2 citation bullets per theme	☑
Gap statement links to matrix data	☑

Ask ChatGPT:

"Rewrite these section headings to use parallel verb-turned-noun phrases under six words."

Or:

"Estimate word count per section if total chapter = 8,000 words, weighted by citation count."

This ensures even depth across themes and prevents over-writing early sections.

Template Outline: Funnel–Thematic Hybrid

I. Introduction
- Contextualize student mental health + rise in social media.
- Define scope: undergraduates, anxiety, platform usage.

II. Patterns of Social Media Use
- Smith (2020): Instagram >3h → anxiety
- Lee (2021): TikTok growth + daily use trends

III. Psychological Outcomes of Use
- Meta-analysis: heavy use ↔ anxiety
- Contrast: some studies show no effect

IV. Moderators and Mediators
- Passive vs. active use
- Self-esteem, peer comparison
- Age and gender effects

V. Gaps and Rationale
- No causal studies in TikTok space
- Lack of American cohort research

VI. Conclusion
- Recap themes and justify your study

Sprint Task (≈ 60 min)

Task	Tool	Deliverable
Choose an outline model	Justify in 50 words (e.g., Funnel–Thematic)	Paste in LitReview_Outline_v1.md
Draft 3–5 top-level headings	Use AI to refine parallel structure	Check with ChatGPT or Grammarly
Add 2–3 citation bullets under each heading	Zotero to Markdown export	Embedded under each section
Write one 40-word gap statement	Base it on Day 11 matrix	Insert in "Gaps" section
Save outline in Obsidian/Notion	Tag as #outline #chapter2	Screenshot or file confirmation

Final Thoughts: The Roadmap Is Now Set

By the end of today, you have:

- ✅ A logic-driven structure
- ✅ Citation-anchored bullets
- ✅ Parallel headings and evidence balance
- ✅ A strategic narrative arc from theme to gap

This outline isn't just a planning tool—it's a **launchpad** for drafting. You now know **what you'll say, where, and why**—making the next stage not just easier, but inevitable.

Day 12 Summary Box

- Today, you move from research analysis to structural design—transforming your thematic findings and gap statements into a clear, logical chapter outline.
- A strong literature review outline balances flow and focus, guiding readers from context to gap using thematic or methodological structure.
- Tools like **Obsidian**, **Notion**, and **Zotero (Better BibTeX)** help you organize citation-linked bullets beneath each section heading.
- Your outline should feature parallel, clearly labeled headings, strategic placement of findings, synthesis insights, and a dedicated section for your research gap and rationale.

Day 13: Set the Stage — Writing the Literature Review Introduction

You've assembled evidence, sorted themes, and mapped connections. Now it's time to begin the actual writing—starting with the **introduction** to your literature review chapter.

This isn't your overall thesis introduction, but the opening paragraph(s) of the *literature review section itself*. Its job? To **motivate, focus, and orient**. In a few well-structured paragraphs, you'll explain why the topic matters, clarify your review's boundaries, and hint at how the chapter unfolds.

A strong introduction makes the rest of your chapter feel inevitable.

Why the Introduction Matters

Think of this opening as your reader's **first step into the forest**. A clear map—where we are, what we're looking for, and how we'll explore—makes everything easier to follow.

A well-written literature review introduction:

- **Frames the relevance** of the topic in current scholarly or social context
- **Narrowly defines** the review's scope (timeframe, population, method)
- **Signals the structure** of your chapter (themes, order, direction)
- **Leads smoothly** into your first body section

According to research from Purdue OWL, Wordvice, and Hull University, literature reviews that start with a structured "funnel to gap" model and include roadmap sentences consistently score higher on clarity, cohesion, and flow (23).

Step-by-Step Structure: From Funnel to Focus

Use this structure to frame your introduction.

1. Broad Context (Funnel Start)

Introduce the general field and explain why it's worth examining.

"Over the past decade, social media has become deeply embedded in the daily lives of young adults, prompting growing concern about its psychological effects."

2. Narrow to Your Topic

Transition into your focus—what exactly this review covers.

"Among these concerns, anxiety has emerged as a key area of investigation, particularly among university students who are heavy users of platforms like Instagram and TikTok."

3. Scope and Delimitations

State what the review *includes* and *excludes* (years, methods, populations).

"This chapter reviews peer-reviewed, quantitative and mixed-methods studies published between 2018 and 2025 focusing on the relationship between social media use and anxiety in undergraduate students."

4. Rationale

Explain why this review is needed—what problem or gap does it address?

"Given the mental health impact of the COVID-19 pandemic and the rapid rise of new platforms, a fresh synthesis of this literature is both timely and necessary."

5. Roadmap Sentence

Tell the reader what to expect in the coming sections—use your thematic outline.

"The chapter is organised into four main sections: usage patterns, psychological outcomes, moderating factors, and identified gaps."

6. Transition to First Section

End with a smooth bridge to Theme 1.

"Understanding how students engage with social media provides a foundation for assessing its potential mental health consequences."

AI Tools: Draft Faster, Polish Better

Task	AI Tool	Prompt Example
Generate a rough draft	ChatGPT	"Write a 500-word funnel-style lit review intro on [topic] using these themes..."
Check heading consistency	ChatGPT	"Rewrite these section headings in parallel gerund form"
Enhance transitions	Wordvice/UNC	Use transition word lists to vary sentence flow
Clarify tone	Grammarly	Academic + Formal + Concise settings
Summarise scope	DiscoverPhDs	Scope templates like: *"This review includes..."*

Example: Complete Draft Introduction

Social media has become a ubiquitous presence in the lives of university students, profoundly shaping how they communicate, consume information, and form identities. Over the past decade, researchers have increasingly explored how these digital interactions intersect with psychological well-being. Among the mental health outcomes studied, anxiety has emerged as a critical concern—particularly in undergraduate populations who engage heavily with platforms such as Instagram, TikTok, and Snapchat.

This literature review examines peer-reviewed, quantitative and mixed-methods studies published between 2018 and 2025 that investigate the relationship between social media use and anxiety in university students. The goal is to synthesize current findings, identify recurring patterns and contradictions, and clarify where research gaps remain. This synthesis is especially relevant in the post-pandemic era, where online engagement has intensified.

The chapter is structured around three major themes: patterns of social media usage, psychological outcomes, and moderating factors. Understanding how students use these platforms provides essential context for exploring their mental health impact.

Sprint Task (≈ 60 min)

Step	Task	Tool / Hint
1	Draft a 500-word introduction using the funnel format	Prompt ChatGPT or Perplexity with outline and scope
2	Write a clear scope/delimitation sentence	Use DiscoverPhDs templates
3	Add a roadmap sentence naming your 3–5 theme headings	Apply UNC or Purdue OWL guide
4	Use 3 formal transitions from Wordvice lists	E.g., *"Moreover," "Conversely," "As a result..."*
5	Save draft as Intro_v1.md in your writing workspace	Tag it #intro #chapter2 for quick reference

Common Pitfalls & Fixes

Pitfall	Fix
Too much general background	Keep the intro to ≤ 10% of chapter word count
No clear scope or timeframe	Include population, time period, and methods in one sentence
Flat or abrupt transitions	Use curated connectors from Wordvice, UNC Writing Center
No link to research question	Reference your refined question or rationale before ending

Final Thoughts: The First Brick Is Laid

Congratulations—you've begun writing.

Your introduction orients your reader, sets expectations, and establishes authority. You now have:

- ✅ A funnel-style intro paragraph
- ✅ A defined scope and timeframe
- ✅ A roadmap sentence connecting themes
- ✅ A transition that guides the reader into your first section

Next, in Day 14, you'll begin drafting the body of your chapter—starting with **Theme 1: Patterns of Social Media Use**.

Now that you've set the stage with a compelling introduction, it's time to dive into the heart of your literature review: the thematic sections. These are where your argument takes shape—through synthesis, comparison, and the strategic layering of evidence. Over the next few days, you'll transform annotated notes and coded themes into coherent narratives that not only summarize what's known, but reveal deeper patterns and scholarly insights. You've laid the foundation—now let's build the core.

Day 13 Summary Box

- The literature review introduction isn't background—it's a strategic on-ramp. Its purpose is to orient the reader, define the review's scope, and preview the chapter's thematic structure.
- Use a **funnel-style structure**: begin with a broad scholarly or societal context, narrow into your specific focus, and conclude with a roadmap sentence.
- Strong introductions include four core elements: topic relevance, scope and delimitations (e.g., years, population), rationale or gap, and an overview of upcoming themes.
- AI tools like **ChatGPT**, **Grammarly**, and **DiscoverPhDs** can accelerate drafting, polish transitions, and refine your academic tone.

Day 13 Checklist: Writing the Literature Review Introduction

Section	Checklist Item	Check
I. Funnel Structure & Focus	Opened with a broad scholarly or societal context to frame the issue	[ ]
	Narrowed the focus to your specific topic, variable, or population	[ ]
	Clearly articulated the scope and delimitations (years, methods, population)	[ ]
	Included a rationale for why this review is timely or needed	[ ]
	Wrote a roadmap sentence outlining the chapter's major thematic sections	[ ]
	Ended with a transition that flows naturally into Theme 1	[ ]
II. Clarity, Style & Tone	Total word count between 500–1000 words or ≤10% of full chapter	[ ]
	Maintained formal, academic, and concise tone throughout	[ ]
	Used at least three academic transition phrases (e.g., "Moreover", "Conversely")	[ ]
	Avoided excessive background or vague generalizations	[ ]
III. Scope Accuracy	Scope sentence includes population, study period, and study types	[ ]
	Clearly identified inclusions and exclusions (e.g., "peer-reviewed studies between 2018–2025")	[ ]
IV. Logical Flow	Paragraphs logically move from general to specific	[ ]
	Sentences flow smoothly with intentional transitions	[ ]
	Final sentence logically bridges into the first body section	[ ]
V. Technical Tools Used	Used ChatGPT or Perplexity to generate a rough intro draft	[ ]
	Used DiscoverPhDs or similar for scope/delimitation sentence templates	[ ]
	Reviewed for tone and clarity with Grammarly, Hemingway, or similar	[ ]
VI. Saving and Tagging	Saved as Intro_v1.md or similar in your writing folder	[ ]
	Tagged the file with #intro and #chapter2 for easy retrieval	[ ]
	Logged version or AI edits for tracking future improvements	[ ]

Day 14: Writing the First Thematic Section — From Notes to Narrative

You've mapped your literature. You've drafted a clear, focused outline. Now comes the turning point—**writing the first thematic section** of your literature review.

This is where your scattered notes, bullet points, and AI summaries begin to form a scholarly argument.

Rather than stacking citations, you'll **synthesize evidence** around a central theme using academic paragraph structure, smooth transitions, and reflective commentary. You're not just reporting what others said—you're showing how the conversation unfolds across sources.

Why This Section Matters

Your first thematic section sets the tone for the rest of the literature review. It shows:

- You can group and interpret evidence meaningfully
- You understand how studies relate to each other
- You're building a case toward a research gap

If written well, this section acts as a **model paragraph** you'll replicate in future themes.

Step-by-Step: Writing with the PEEL Framework

Use the **PEEL** (24) or **TEEL** (25) structure, a proven academic writing scaffold:

Component	Description	Example
Point	Start with a topic sentence stating the main idea	"College students report high daily use of social media platforms."
Evidence	Provide specific findings from 2–3 studies	"Smith (2020) found an average of 2.5 hours/day on Instagram..."
Explanation	Compare, contrast, interpret, or explain significance	"These findings reflect a consistent trend, though Chen (2019) found lower use among Asian students."
Link	End with a sentence leading to the next section or theme	"These usage patterns provide the necessary backdrop for exploring how such use relates to anxiety."

Tip: Keep each PEEL paragraph focused on one micro-theme. If needed, write **two paragraphs per main theme**.

Example Paragraph

Point: *Undergraduate students spend considerable time on social media each day, often across multiple platforms.*

Evidence: *Smith (2020) surveyed 200 US students and found Instagram use averaged 2.5 hours/day. Similarly, Lee (2021) reported an average of 1.8 hours/day on Facebook among UK undergraduates. In contrast, Chen (2019) found only 1 hour/day of usage among students in Singapore, indicating regional variance.*

Explanation: *This pattern suggests that while social media is a consistent part of student life globally, cultural and platform-specific differences influence duration and engagement.*

Link: *These usage behaviors provide a foundation for examining how social media exposure may contribute to student anxiety—an issue explored in the next section.*

AI-Assisted Writing Workflow

Here's how to go from outline to paragraph using digital tools:

Step	Tool	Prompt
Draft a topic sentence	ChatGPT or Perplexity	"Write a topic sentence summarizing studies on social media use patterns among students."
Generate evidence bullets	Zotero → Markdown export	Use citation snippets like *Smith 2020: 2.5 hrs/day Instagram*
Build a paragraph	ChatGPT	"Turn these bullets into a PEEL paragraph, with comparisons and transitions."
Refine style	Grammarly or SciSpace	Adjust tone, grammar, clarity
Check citation logic	scite.ai plugin	Flag "contrasting" evidence and update paragraph tone accordingly

Writing Tips and Transitions

Purpose	Examples
Add evidence	"Additionally," "For example," "Likewise"
Show contrast	"However," "In contrast," "Despite this"
Explain significance	"This suggests," "These findings imply," "Such data indicates"
Link forward	"This trend sets the stage for…", "This issue leads us to…"

Sprint Task (≈ 60 min)

Task	Deliverable
1. Draft 1–2 paragraphs for Theme 1 using PEEL format	≤ 250 words per paragraph
2. Insert in-text citations for 2–3 studies	E.g., *Smith (2020), Lee (2021)*
3. Highlight transitions in yellow	Check for flow and avoid repetition
4. Use scite badges to label supporting vs contrasting sources	Mark contrasting evidence in red
5. Optional: Swap for peer review (or use ChatGPT review prompt)	"Critique this paragraph: suggest improvements for logic, clarity, and citation balance."
6. Write a short memo on what you revised and why	100 words; reflect on synthesis and transitions

Common Pitfalls & Fixes

Pitfall	Fix
Listing studies without comparison	Use synthesis connectors like *"whereas"*, *"similarly"*

Over-quoting or summarizing entire studies	Focus on 1–2 key data points per study
Repeating transitions	Vary structure using curated phrase lists
AI citation hallucination	Verify with Zotero + scite plugin or DOI search

Final Thoughts: From Plan to Paragraph

You've now written your first thematic section—a real milestone in your literature review journey.

- ✅ Your ideas are structured
- ✅ Your sources are synthesized
- ✅ Your narrative is progressing

This section isn't just informative—it's persuasive. You're building the groundwork for your research argument, paragraph by paragraph.

Day 14 Summary Box

- Begin drafting your first **thematic body section** using a clear, structured academic format (e.g., PEEL).
- Focus on **synthesis**, not summary—compare, contrast, and interpret findings across 2–3 studies per paragraph.
- Use the **PEEL structure**:
    - **Point**: Introduce the micro-theme or claim.
    - **Evidence**: Present brief, relevant findings from key studies.
    - **Explanation**: Analyze and connect those findings, highlighting patterns or contradictions.
    - **Link**: Transition to the next theme or paragraph logically.
- Prioritize **clarity and flow**: each paragraph should center on one main idea and logically lead to the next.
- Use **transition words** to strengthen cohesion (e.g., "In contrast," "This trend suggests," "Consequently").
- Support your evidence base with tools like **scite.ai** to identify supporting vs. contrasting citations.
- Use AI tools (ChatGPT, Perplexity) to draft topic sentences, build paragraph scaffolds, and improve phrasing.
- Ensure in-text citations are embedded cleanly (APA or your required style), using Zotero export or plugins.

Day 14 Checklist: Writing the First Thematic Section (Theme 1)

Category	Checklist Item	Check
I. Paragraph Structure (PEEL)	Paragraph opens with a clear Point/topic sentence that introduces the micro-theme	[ ]
	Includes 2–3 pieces of evidence from different studies (with citations)	[ ]
	Provides comparative explanation that interprets or contrasts findings	[ ]
	Ends with a linking sentence that bridges to the next theme or paragraph	[ ]
	Paragraph stays focused on one core idea	[ ]
II. Citation & Source Quality	At least two in-text citations are provided using correct formatting	[ ]
	Evidence includes both supporting and contrasting findings where available	[ ]
	Used scite.ai or equivalent to flag the strength of sources (supporting vs. contrasting)	[ ]
	Confirmed study details using Zotero, DOI, or full-text PDF	[ ]
III. Cohesion & Flow	Used appropriate transition words (e.g., "Moreover," "However," "This suggests...")	[ ]
	Varied transitions across paragraphs to avoid repetition	[ ]
	Maintained clear logic and sequence across sentences	[ ]
	Final sentence creates a natural bridge to the next theme	[ ]
IV. AI & Writing Tools	Used ChatGPT or Perplexity to help generate a topic sentence or full draft	[ ]
	Refined grammar and tone with Grammarly, SciSpace, or Hemingway	[ ]
	Paragraph reviewed and revised for clarity, flow, and scholarly tone	[ ]
V. Reflection & Revision	Saved the paragraph in your writing folder as Theme1_v1.md or similar	[ ]
	Highlighted transition phrases in yellow for review	[ ]
	Optional: Peer-reviewed or used ChatGPT to critique paragraph logic and balance	[ ]
	Wrote a short 100-word memo on what you revised and why	[ ]

Day 15: Writing the Second Thematic Section

By now, your literature review is taking form. In Day 14, you built momentum by writing your first thematic section. In this chapter, we write the second thematic section by tackling the **core issue** in our review example: the relationship between **social media use and anxiety**.

This isn't just a descriptive task. It's our first deep analytical dive. The section should highlight points of agreement, surface contradictions, and weigh the **strength of evidence**, while keeping the reader oriented with smooth transitions.

Why This Section Matters

This is likely the **heart of your literature review**—the theme most closely tied to your research question. Readers (and reviewers) will judge the strength of your synthesis here. So, don't just summarize—**synthesize**, **compare**, and **evaluate**.

You're not trying to include every study—you're trying to create an argument about what the collective evidence suggests.

Step 1: Frame the Theme with a Strong Opening

Use the **PEEL structure** (Point, Evidence, Explanation, Link) to anchor your section. Your topic sentence should:

- Signal the theme
- Summarize the pattern in literature (e.g., "positive link," "mixed findings")
- Narrow to your cohort (e.g., undergraduates, adolescents)

Example:
"Recent research linking social media use to anxiety among university students shows a generally positive association, though not without exceptions."

Step 2: Present and Compare the Evidence

Cluster your sources. Highlight converging findings first, then introduce contrasting ones. Vary sentence starters and use transition phrases (e.g., *Similarly, However, Collectively*).

Study	Finding	Method Note
Smith (2020)	+20% anxiety for Instagram >3h/day	Self-report survey
Lee (2021)	Stress scores higher for heavy Facebook users	Survey with stratified sampling
Chen (2019)	No significant difference after sleep control	Regression with covariates
Jones (2022)	Stronger effect for active vs passive use	Longitudinal tracking study

Use PEEL:

1. *Point*: Students using social media heavily often report higher anxiety.
2. *Evidence*: Smith (2020) and Lee (2021) found 15–20% increased symptoms.
3. *Explanation*: This pattern suggests dose-response logic, though platform design and self-reporting methods may skew precision.
4. *Link*: Yet not all findings align, and methodological nuance helps explain the divergence.

Step 3: Highlight Methodological Differences

Differentiate survey studies from experimental or digital-tracking ones. Explain how **study design**, **measurement tools**, or **controls** influence outcomes.

Example:
"Jones (2022) used passive data logging, avoiding recall bias, while Chen (2019) relied on self-reports and showed weaker associations."

Bonus: Flag studies in **scite.ai** with "contrasting" badges, and comment on their outlier status.

Step 4: Conclude with a Transition to the Next Theme

Your closing sentence should wrap up this theme **and hint at the complexities ahead**—e.g., mediators like self-esteem, content type, or usage style.

Example:
"While the weight of evidence suggests a correlation between heavy social media use and elevated anxiety levels, the variability in outcomes points to deeper mechanisms—such as how users engage with content—explored in the next section."

Sample Synthesized Paragraph

Surveys consistently report a link between high social media use and increased anxiety among undergraduates. Smith (2020) found that students spending over three hours daily on Instagram had 20% higher anxiety scores compared to light users. Similarly, Lee (2021) observed elevated stress among heavy Facebook users. However, Chen (2019), controlling for sleep and exercise, found no significant difference in anxiety across usage levels. Methodology may explain these discrepancies: Jones (2022), using digital activity logs over 30 days, confirmed anxiety increased with passive scrolling but not active engagement. These patterns suggest that not just time online, but how students interact with platforms, may influence outcomes—a distinction examined further in the next section.

Common Mistakes to Avoid

Pitfall	Fix
Just listing studies	Always compare and explain why results differ
Overreliance on surveys	Acknowledge method limitations (recall bias, self-reporting)
Weak transitions	Vary with cause/effect, contrast, and addition signals
AI citation hallucinations	Cross check every source with Zotero or DOI

Sprint Task (≈ 60 minutes)

Step	Task	Tool / Deliverable
1	Draft 1–2 PEEL paragraphs (250–300 words total)	Theme2_draft.md
2	Use transition phrases from Wordvice/UNC	Highlight transitions in yellow
3	Flag at least one contrasting study from scite.ai	Red text in Zotero
4	Run your paragraph through ChatGPT "critical reviewer" prompt	"Identify logical flaws and suggest 1 improvement."
5	Write a 100-word reflection on what you revised	Revision_memo.md

Sample Peer Review Prompt (ChatGPT)

"Act as a critical reviewer. Review the following literature paragraph for coherence, flow, citation use, and balance of evidence. Suggest one concrete improvement."

Final Thought

By the end of today, you've written the **analytical core** of your chapter. You've not only presented what the literature says—you've demonstrated your ability to **interpret, contrast, and explain it**.

Next, in Day 16, we'll unpack the **contradictions, debates, and complexities**—turning academic ambiguity into scholarly insight.

Stay sharp—you're halfway through your literature sprint.

Day 15 Summary Box

- Focus today on writing **Theme 2**, the core issue of your review: how social media use correlates with anxiety among your target population.
- Use the **PEEL structure** to guide paragraph construction:
    - **Point**: Open with a topic sentence framing the general trend (e.g., "Studies show a positive link...").
    - **Evidence**: Cite 2–3 key studies showing converging or diverging results.
    - **Explanation**: Interpret differences—especially based on study design or methodology.
    - **Link**: Transition to the next paragraph or theme (e.g., exploring mechanisms).
- **Cluster your findings**: Present converging evidence first, then address outliers or contradictions.
- Use **methodological analysis** to explain discrepancies (e.g., survey vs. digital tracking).
- Apply tools like **scite.ai** to flag and discuss contrasting or weakly supported findings.
- End with a **bridge sentence** to the next theme, pointing to mediators like content type or user behavior.
- Draft **1–2 full paragraphs (250–300 words total)** with clear transitions and balanced citations.
- Avoid stacking summaries—always compare, contrast, and reflect on study quality or context.
- Use ChatGPT or Grammarly to refine structure, style, and citation coherence.

Day 16: Addressing Contradictions and Debates

Welcome to Day 16—the day your literature review gains **depth and credibility**. So far, you've presented individual themes and trends. Now it's time to **acknowledge the messiness**: the studies that conflict, contradict, or complicate the narrative. This is where you demonstrate *real* scholarly thinking.

Rather than viewing contradictions as a flaw, treat them as **valuable signals**: they show where the literature is contested, how methodology shapes outcomes, and why your own research question is timely.

Why Contradictions Matter

A strong literature review does *not* cherry-pick only confirming studies. Instead, it:

- Demonstrates mastery of the field
- Shows fairness and critical thinking
- Builds a persuasive case for *why your study is needed*

Openly analyzing disagreement boosts a review's **trustworthiness**. Reviewers *expect* to see debates.

Step 1: Spot Contradictions in Your Notes

Review your literature matrix or theme summaries and identify points where:

Topic	One study says...	Another says...	Possible reason
Time on Instagram	↑ Anxiety (Smith, 2020)	No effect (Chen, 2019)	Measurement & personality controls
Content type	Passive use = worse (Meta-Analysis, 2024)	Posting = better mood (Lee, 2021)	Activity type & context
Method used	Self-report shows strong link	Device log shows weaker effect	Recall bias vs actual behavior

Use these juxtapositions as the basis for your argument.

Step 2: Write a PEEL-Structured Debate Paragraph

Follow the **Point–Evidence–Explanation–Link** structure for each contradiction you present.

Sample Paragraph

While most studies link social media use to elevated anxiety, not all findings align. Smith (2020) reported that Instagram use over 3 hours per day was associated with a 20% increase in anxiety scores among U.S. undergraduates. However, Chen (2019) found no significant relationship in a Chinese cohort after controlling for personality traits. This difference may stem from ***measurement methods****—Smith used* ***self-reports****, while Chen relied on* ***device-tracked screen time****—and from* ***sample characteristics*** *like cultural norms and sleep patterns. Supporting this, Jones (2022) found that self-reported screen time overestimated use by nearly twofold. Moreover, Lee (2021) found that sharing positive content could actually* ***lower*** *anxiety levels, contradicting passive scrolling effects identified in the 2024 meta-analysis. These contradictions suggest that the link between social media and anxiety may depend more on how and why platforms are used than on usage time alone.* ***This complexity highlights the need to explore mediating factors—such as content type and user intent—which remain understudied.***

Step 3: Use AI Tools to Support Synthesis

AI-Powered Table Prompt

Ask ChatGPT:

"Create a 4-column table comparing two studies that support and two that contradict the claim 'social media increases anxiety,' including sample size, population, measurement type, and findings."

Verify the sources in Zotero or Crossref. Then export the table into your literature matrix or appendix.

Step 4: Link the Debate to the Gap

Your final sentence should gently nudge the reader toward the **unresolved questions** or **research gaps**—the ones *your study* will soon address.

Example:
"These methodological and contextual inconsistencies point to the need for more nuanced, longitudinal research into social media content and user intent—gaps addressed in the next section."

Sprint Task Instructions (≈ 60 min)

Task	Deliverable
Write 1 PEEL paragraph (200–250 words) comparing ≥3 supporting and 2 contradicting studies	Theme2_Debate.md
Bold the drivers of divergence (method, sample, measure)	Inline in paragraph
Create a comparison table in AI or Excel	Add to your matrix
Use a transition from UNC's list to move between studies	Highlight transitions in yellow
End with a clear gap lead-out sentence (≤ 25 words)	✓
Self-review: Revise any repeated transitions and write a 50-word memo	Revision_Memo.md

Suggested ChatGPT Prompts

- *"Write a debate-style paragraph comparing studies with opposing results on social media use and anxiety, using PEEL format."*
- *"Suggest 3 transitions to introduce conflicting studies in an academic paragraph."*
- *"Create a table comparing four studies on social media use and anxiety: two supporting and two contradicting."*

Closing Thought

This section separates descriptive writers from analytical thinkers. By **acknowledging contradictions** and **exploring possible reasons**, you build scholarly credibility—and lay the foundation for your study's relevance.

Next, in Day 17, you'll tie it all together with a compelling **literature review conclusion**.

You've done a brilliant job synthesizing complexity—keep going!

Day 16 Summary Box

- Today's focus is on **critically analyzing conflicting findings**—transforming inconsistencies in the literature into scholarly insight.
- Contradictions should be **framed as valuable signals**, not problems—they reveal the boundaries, gaps, and methodological tensions in your field.
- Begin by reviewing your notes and literature matrix to **identify conflicting studies** (e.g., differences in population, design, measures).
- Use the **PEEL structure** to craft a paragraph:
    - **Point**: Acknowledge the contradiction.
    - **Evidence**: Present at least two studies with opposing findings.
    - **Explanation**: Analyze potential causes—e.g., study design, self-report vs. log data, cultural factors.
    - **Link**: End by connecting the contradiction to a broader insight or segue into the next theme.
- **Highlight methodological contrasts** (e.g., self-report vs. tracking, Western vs. non-Western populations) to explain divergence.
- Use tools like **ChatGPT**, **scite.ai**, and **Zotero** to support evidence gathering and verify citation reliability.
- Create a **comparison table** (supporting vs. contradicting studies) to visualize the debate in your literature matrix.
- End the paragraph with a **lead-in sentence to your next section** (e.g., user intent or content as a mediating factor).
- Avoid common pitfalls like over-reliance on one perspective or skipping transitions—strive for **balance and nuance**.
- This section is where you demonstrate **critical thinking and academic maturity**—a key marker of a strong literature review.

Day 17: Synthesizing the Story: Writing the Literature Review Conclusion

By Day 17, you've combed through the literature, identified patterns and debates, mapped thematic trajectories, and clarified where your work fits. The task now is to write the final section of your literature review: a concise, coherent conclusion that reinforces your contribution, sharpens your research gap, and transitions gracefully into your methodology.

Why the Conclusion Matters

In a well-structured literature review, the conclusion is not a mere summary—it's the pivot point. It must bring intellectual closure to the chapter while opening a door into your study. Think of it as completing the "funnel" structure that began in your introduction: from general context to targeted insight, culminating in a precise rationale for your research.

1. Synthesize, Don't Repeat

Begin by revisiting your major thematic insights in a synthesized format. This means summarizing—not re-listing—the overarching findings and tensions. You are now the guide, showing your reader the key contours of the terrain you've just mapped.

Example:
"Collectively, the literature suggests a consistent association between frequent social media use and elevated anxiety levels among university students, especially on image-centric platforms. However, the strength of this relationship varies across contexts and measurement tools."

Be careful not to introduce new citations or evidence at this point. Your goal is synthesis and signposting, not further exploration.

2. Restate the Research Gap

Next, return to the gap you identified earlier (Day 11). But do so with greater clarity and purpose. Now that the reader understands the field's contours, your gap should feel urgent and well-founded.

Example:
"Despite the growing body of research, there remains a notable lack of longitudinal studies examining the psychological effects of TikTok use among students in American university settings."

Make sure your gap echoes the themes you've already developed—not a surprise detour. A well-framed gap signals that your study is not just timely, but necessary.

3. Justify the Significance

After stating the gap, explain why it matters. This can be done in a sentence or two. Connect the literature's limitations to real-world trends, theoretical developments, or policy needs.

Example:
"As TikTok rapidly becomes the dominant social media platform among Generation Z, understanding its psychological effects—particularly in diverse cultural contexts—is critical to informing mental health strategies on campus and beyond."

This is your opportunity to highlight the stakes of your work—intellectual, practical, or both.

4. Lead into Your Research

Finally, conclude the chapter by stating how your own research will respond to the identified gap. This is not your full research proposal—just a glimpse of the road ahead.

Example:
"The current study addresses this gap by employing a mixed-methods design to track anxiety outcomes among first-year American university students over a full academic year."

This move transitions your reader logically and persuasively into your methodology chapter. It signals that the literature review has done its job: it has mapped the field, identified a need, and set the stage for new inquiry.

Recap: Four Moves of a Literature Review Conclusion

Move	Purpose
1. Synthesize	Recap major themes and contradictions from the review
2. Restate the Gap	Clearly and concisely frame the unresolved issue
3. Explain the Significance	Justify why the gap matters and who it affects
4. Lead Forward	Preview how your research addresses the gap

Final Thoughts

Many doctoral students undervalue the conclusion, seeing it as a formality. But a well-written literature review conclusion can leave a lasting impression—clarifying your scholarly vision and positioning your study as the logical next step in the field.

You've now closed the chapter, both literally and structurally. In the next phase, you'll build on this foundation to articulate your research design, align your questions with methods, and define the boundaries of your empirical inquiry.

Next Steps

- Review your thematic codebook from Days 9–11 to ensure alignment with your gap.

- Draft a 150–200 word conclusion using the four-move structure.
- Insert it into your working literature review draft and link it to your planned methodology section outline.

When you're ready, we'll begin transforming Day 18—"Final Review and Polishing"—into a chapter that helps you edit for flow, logic, and scholarly tone.

Day 17 Summary Box

- Today's focus is on writing a cohesive conclusion that synthesizes your literature review and clearly sets up your research rationale.
- A strong conclusion does not simply summarize—it connects themes, clarifies contradictions, and highlights the unresolved gap.
- Use the **Four-Move Model**:

    1. **Synthesize** main findings across themes without repeating all citations.
    2. **Restate the gap** using concise, evidence-backed phrasing.
    3. **Explain the significance** of this gap in scholarly, practical, or policy terms.
    4. **Lead forward** by previewing how your study addresses the issue.

- Avoid adding new sources or data; this section should distill and direct, not expand.
- This paragraph transitions the reader smoothly from literature to methodology.

PART IV: POLISH AND FINALIZE

Day 18: Paraphrasing and Citing Properly

As you move from gathering and synthesizing literature to articulating your own position, few academic skills matter more than paraphrasing effectively and citing ethically. These practices are not merely about avoiding plagiarism; they lie at the heart of scholarly integrity. A well-crafted paraphrase shows that you understand your source deeply enough to reframe it in your own voice. A well-placed citation signals that you're part of an academic dialogue—not merely consuming knowledge but building on it.

By Day 18, your literature review is already rich with ideas drawn from diverse sources. Today's focus is to ensure those ideas are properly represented and clearly distinguished from your own. That means learning how to restate others' work in fresh, accurate language and to attribute it in a way that meets both the letter and the spirit of academic conventions.

Why Paraphrasing Is Not Just Rewording

Paraphrasing often gets mistaken for simply replacing a few words with synonyms. In fact, true paraphrasing involves reprocessing meaning. You must first understand the idea, pause to reflect on its core insight, and then recast it as if explaining it to someone else from scratch. This internalization is what transforms a borrowed idea into one that feels organically embedded in your narrative. It also strengthens your writing voice—one of the most undervalued tools of academic persuasion.

Consider the following original sentence:

"Students who spend more than 3 hours on Instagram daily are more likely to report elevated anxiety symptoms."

A lazy paraphrase might look like this:

"Learners using Instagram over 3 hours each day tend to show increased signs of anxiety."

While this avoids identical wording, it does little to demonstrate understanding. A thoughtful paraphrase, however, might say:

"High-frequency Instagram users—defined as those online for more than three hours a day—report greater levels of anxiety, according to recent survey-based findings (Smith, 2020)."

Here, the sentence has been structurally altered and enriched with contextual detail, all while clearly attributing the claim.

The Gold Standard: Paraphrasing in Six Steps

Adapting guidance from the Purdue OWL and writing centers across major universities, the following six-step method ensures that your paraphrasing is both accurate and original (26):

- **Read the passage carefully** until you fully understand its meaning.
- **Set the source aside** to avoid unconscious mimicry.
- **Rephrase the idea** as if explaining it to a peer in your own words.
- **Check your version** against the original to confirm accuracy and to eliminate unintended overlap in phrasing.
- **Insert a citation** immediately—even if your draft is still rough. This habit prevents lost attribution later.
- **Use quotation marks** for any exact words or phrases you retain, and explain why they're preserved.

Practicing these steps consistently not only sharpens your prose but also reinforces your confidence in academic writing. You begin to trust your own language, even when describing the work of others.

Citing with Clarity: APA Style in Practice

Once you've paraphrased, your next responsibility is citation. In APA 7 style—used across most social sciences and health disciplines—there are two standard citation formats:

- **Narrative citation**: Smith (2020) reported that...
- **Parenthetical citation**: ...as found in several studies (Smith, 2020).

Both are equally acceptable and should be chosen based on the flow of your sentence. More important than format, however, is placement: cite as close as possible to the paraphrased content to avoid ambiguity. If your paragraph integrates multiple sources, ensure each idea is clearly connected to its citation.

Quoting vs. Paraphrasing: Making the Right Call

Use direct quotes sparingly. They are best reserved for definitions, technical language, or particularly eloquent phrases that would lose nuance if altered. For everything else, paraphrasing is preferred—it demonstrates mastery and helps maintain a cohesive narrative tone. If you must quote, integrate it smoothly into your sentence and always include a page number:

"This pattern of use reflects a 'platform-mediated form of emotional labor' (Ahmed, 2021, p. 94)."

For summary-level references—such as when describing the overall conclusion of a meta-analysis—citing the entire work with a paraphrased overview is sufficient.

Paraphrasing with AI: Aid, Not Authority

AI tools like ChatGPT or QuillBot can be useful for generating paraphrase drafts. You might paste a sentence into your tool of choice and ask: "Can you rephrase this in a more concise academic tone?"

However, treat AI as a collaborator, not an oracle. It cannot assess the accuracy of the paraphrase in relation to the original study's intent. Always verify, refine, and add your own context. Think of it as scaffolding—not a finished wall.

Similarly, plagiarism detection tools like Turnitin or Grammarly's citation checker can help surface overly similar phrasing or forgotten attributions. But they are not infallible. Their output should support—not substitute—your editorial judgment.

Finalizing Your References

Every in-text citation should correspond to a complete entry in your reference list. As you move toward the editing phase of your literature review, this is a good time to ensure consistency. If you're using Zotero, Mendeley, or EndNote, exporting your bibliography with one click will save hours of formatting later. Most reference managers now offer "Quick Copy" or "Cite While You Write" features that ensure a tight link between in-text and end-of-text citations.

Closing Reflection

Paraphrasing and citing are not mechanical chores; they're intellectual acts. They show your reader—and your examiner—that you understand the material, respect the scholarly lineage behind your topic, and are ready to make your own contribution to that conversation. When you paraphrase well, your literature review becomes not just a summary of what others have said, but a launchpad for your own research agenda.

On Day 19, we'll begin revisiting your chapter holistically—starting with polishing transitions and checking for coherence across sections. But for today, pause to appreciate the scholarly fluency you've been developing. Every citation placed correctly, every paraphrase reworded meaningfully, is a step toward becoming not just a reader of research, but a creator of it.

Next Steps:

- Review three paragraphs from your current draft. Check that every paraphrased idea includes a citation, and rewrite any sentence that leans too closely on original phrasing.
- Generate a summary of your top five cited sources with one paraphrased sentence each.
- Open your reference manager and confirm that each in-text citation matches a full reference entry.

Day 18 Summary Box

- Today focuses on paraphrasing accurately and citing responsibly—core pillars of scholarly integrity.
- Effective paraphrasing means fully understanding an idea, then restating it in your own academic voice—not just swapping synonyms.
- Use the **six-step paraphrasing method**: understand → set aside → rephrase → check accuracy → cite → quote only if necessary.
- Apply **APA 7 style** consistently—use narrative or parenthetical citations, depending on flow, and always cite close to the paraphrased content.
- Use **quotes sparingly**, only for definitions, technical phrases, or eloquent wording that would lose precision if changed.
- AI tools (e.g., ChatGPT, QuillBot) can assist in paraphrasing drafts, but must be reviewed for accuracy and ethical use.
- Reference managers (Zotero, EndNote, Mendeley) streamline citation formatting and help maintain consistency across in-text and full references.

Day 19: Using Reference Management Software

Let the Machine Do the Formatting—You Focus on the Thinking

At this point in your literature review journey, you've read deeply, synthesized wisely, paraphrased responsibly, and cited ethically. Now it's time to bring structure and polish to your referencing using tools that were designed to take the drudgery out of academic formatting. Enter the reference manager—a quiet workhorse that automates citations, organizes your sources, and ensures your final chapter aligns with scholarly expectations.

Many researchers, especially in the early stages of graduate work, struggle with the tail-end mechanics of referencing. The commas, italics, parentheses, and punctuation points required by citation styles like APA or Chicago can seem like a trap door beneath otherwise solid writing. But the truth is: you no longer have to format anything manually. With the right software setup, reference lists update in real-time, citation styles can be changed in seconds, and your bibliography becomes a clean, coherent artifact of your academic process—not a dreaded postscript.

Why Reference Managers Are Non-Negotiable

Reference managers like **Zotero**, **Mendeley**, **EndNote**, or **Paperpile** aren't optional tools in modern graduate research—they're standard infrastructure. They allow you to:

- Insert properly formatted in-text citations as you write.
- Automatically generate your reference list or bibliography.
- Seamlessly switch between citation styles with a single click.

- Maintain a searchable, tagged database of every source you've read, cited, or discarded.

Moreover, they reduce citation errors—often the first thing examiners and reviewers will notice—and make future papers easier to build because your entire literature trail is archived and accessible.

Choosing the Right Tool for You

Each major reference manager has its strengths:

- **Zotero** is free, open-source, and well-integrated with Word, LibreOffice, and Google Docs. It excels at syncing across devices and supports over 10,000 citation styles via the CSL repository.
- **Mendeley** pairs tightly with Word (especially in Windows environments) and has powerful PDF annotation tools.
- **EndNote**, though pricier, is popular for large collaborative libraries and publication-specific templates.
- **Paperpile** is ideal for Google Docs users, especially those working in browser-based environments like Chromebooks.

No matter which tool you choose, the workflow is largely the same: build your library, insert citations as you write, and generate a formatted bibliography at the end.

Setting Up and Integrating

Once your preferred software is installed, make sure you connect it to your writing environment:

- For **Word**, install the plugin that places an "Add Citation" button directly into your toolbar.
- For **Google Docs**, Zotero and Paperpile both offer browser-based integration that works seamlessly via sidebars or pop-up search boxes.

Now, as you move through your draft, you can simply click "Add/Edit Citation," search for the author or title, and insert an in-text reference like *(Smith, 2020)* in APA style. Better still, you can toggle to MLA, Vancouver, or Chicago with one style change at the end—no manual edits required.

Building Your Bibliography: The One-Click Finale

Once all your citations are in place, generating your bibliography is as simple as clicking "Add Bibliography" or "Insert References." The software pulls every cited work into a clean, alphabetized list, formatted precisely to the chosen style. This ensures your references are not only complete but consistent—a crucial mark of academic professionalism.

Still, trust but verify: always scan your generated bibliography for anomalies. Watch for:

- Author names with inconsistent capitalization.
- Article titles that appear in sentence case vs. title case (especially in APA).
- Missing fields like volume, issue number, or page range.

Most citation errors arise not from the manager itself but from incomplete metadata in your imported entries. A quick manual review can resolve these.

Power Tips for Managing Your Library

To further enhance your workflow, consider these advanced practices:

- **Merge Duplicates**: In Zotero, go to *Duplicate Items*, select the entries, and click *Merge*. This cleans up your reference list and ensures each citation points to a single record.
- **RTF Scan**: If you've drafted your review in plain text or LaTeX, use the "RTF Scan" feature to retroactively convert placeholder citations (like {Smith, 2020}) into formatted references.

- **Quick Copy and citekeys**: For Markdown or Obsidian users, enable "Better BibTeX" to quickly insert citekeys like [@smith2020] and auto-generate reference files on export.
- **Cloud Backup**: Zotero offers free 300MB cloud sync, but you can expand this using WebDAV or Google Drive integration. A cloud-synced library protects against data loss and enables multi-device access.

Quality Assurance: The Final Check

Before moving on, ensure that your reference manager is fully doing its job:

- **Hover over citations** in your draft to preview metadata—confirm that authors, years, and titles match your expectations.
- **Test citation styles** by switching to a different format and back (e.g., APA to Chicago). If the citations update automatically without red flags or errors, you're using active field codes—not static text.
- **Cross-check your bibliography** against your in-text citations. Every cited work should appear once, and only once, at the end.

Reflecting Forward

Reference management is more than a technical task—it's a sign that your research practice is mature, organized, and reproducible. By embedding good citation habits and software skills now, you're building a writing environment that will serve you not just through your PhD, but into publication, collaboration, and policy contribution.

A Word on Citation Ethics

It's worth closing with a brief reminder about *why* we cite. Citations aren't just about obeying formalities—they're about intellectual transparency. They reveal where your ideas came from, invite others into the conversation, and give credit where it's due. Don't over-cite to pad your list, and don't under-cite to imply originality where there is none. Use your reference manager to stay accurate, not manipulative.

Next, we begin the final editing phase: polishing your prose, improving transitions, and tightening the logical flow across sections. But for today, you've brought your draft into full scholarly form—tagged, tracked, and reference-ready.

Next Steps

- Open your literature review draft and insert all missing in-text citations using your reference manager's plugin.
- Generate a complete bibliography using your chosen citation style.
- Run a duplicate check and clean your Zotero (or equivalent) library.
- Back up your library to the cloud or export a .bib or .ris file for safekeeping.
- Perform a style-swap test: try switching from APA to Chicago and back. Observe whether formatting holds.

You've now reached the stage where your references carry their own weight—meticulously organized, automatically styled, and entirely under your control.

Day 19 Summary Box

- Today you focus on setting up and mastering a reference manager like **Zotero, Mendeley, EndNote,** or **Paperpile**—turning your citation process into an efficient, error-free workflow.
- Reference managers **automate citation formatting**, reduce manual errors, and allow you to switch styles (e.g., APA → Chicago) with one click.
- Tools like **Zotero's Word/Google Docs plugin** enable you to insert citations as you write and build a live bibliography that updates automatically.
- Cleaning your library (e.g., merging duplicates) and checking metadata ensures a **professional, accurate reference list**.
- For advanced users, features like **RTF scan, citekeys for Obsidian,** and **cloud backup** (via WebDAV or Google Drive) enhance flexibility and security.
- Final checklist includes: inserting all citations, generating a bibliography, verifying formatting, testing style-switching, and backing up your library.

Day 20: Enhancing Writing Style and Flow

By Day 20 of your literature review journey, you've likely amassed a draft that is coherent, evidence-rich, and structurally sound. But strong academic writing doesn't stop at getting the ideas right—it must also *sound right*. The difference between a draft that merely presents research and one that persuades, engages, and earns citations lies in style and flow.

In this chapter, we focus on refining your prose so it's not only accurate but also elegant. That means ensuring your paragraphs flow smoothly, your sentences are crisp and varied, your voice is active and assured, and your transitions guide the reader effortlessly from one idea to the next.

Why Style Matters in Academic Writing

Academic prose often suffers from a reputation for being dense or inaccessible. Yet, the best literature reviews read with clarity and conviction. Style is not superficial; it shapes how your argument is received. Clear and confident writing reflects mastery of the subject, and well-structured prose earns trust.

Moreover, research shows that readability scores—such as Flesch-Kincaid—are predictive of peer review success, article downloads, and even citation counts. Reviewers, supervisors, and future readers all benefit from writing that is easy to follow and free from unnecessary complexity.

Five Core Strategies to Improve Style and Flow

Let's walk through five research-backed techniques that will elevate your writing from "technically fine" to "professionally polished."

Read Your Work Aloud

This timeless revision strategy works because the ear catches awkward phrasing the eye overlooks. When read aloud, overly long sentences, confusing syntax, or clunky transitions reveal themselves. If you're not comfortable reading to someone else, use a text-to-speech tool built into Word, Google Docs, or third-party apps. Mark anything that sounds off, then revise it for clarity.

Prefer Active Voice

Academic writing has traditionally tolerated passive constructions, but that doesn't mean they're ideal. Consider:

- *Passive*: "It was found that students using Instagram felt more anxious."
- *Active*: "Researchers found that students using Instagram felt more anxious."

The active voice is more concise, more engaging, and assigns clear agency to researchers or authors. Aim for 70% or more of your prose to be in active voice. Tools like Grammarly or Paperpal can flag passive sentences for revision.

Vary Sentence Length and Structure

Monotony in sentence structure fatigues the reader. If all your sentences are long, complex, and similarly constructed, your prose will drag. Conversely, short sentences used too frequently can feel abrupt.

A good rhythm mixes sentence lengths. For example:

"Instagram is used daily by over 70% of college students. But use alone isn't the issue. Recent studies suggest it's the *type* of use—passive scrolling versus interactive engagement—that matters most."

This variation enhances readability and energy.

Trim Filler Words

Clarity often means saying more with fewer words. Phrases like "very," "really," "actually," "in order to," or "it is important to note that" can usually be cut without loss. Review each paragraph and challenge every word: does it earn its place?

- "It is important to note that researchers have found..." becomes "Researchers have found..."
- "In order to examine" becomes simply "To examine."

Concise writing is more powerful writing.

Use Transitions Thoughtfully

Transitions are the glue that hold your argument together. Words like "However," "Moreover," "In contrast," and "As a result" help your reader follow your reasoning and anticipate shifts in focus.

Each paragraph should begin with a topic sentence and end with a line that either closes the point or leads into the next. If your ideas feel disjointed, it may be a signal that transitions need strengthening or paragraphs need reordering.

Here are a few common transition types:

Purpose	Examples
Addition	Moreover, Furthermore, In addition
Contrast	However, On the other hand, Nonetheless
Cause and Effect	Therefore, As a result, Consequently
Clarification	In other words, That is, Namely
Example or Emphasis	For instance, In particular, Especially

Avoid overusing any single transition type. Variety supports flow.

Digital Tools to Aid Revision

While you should trust your own voice, a few AI-powered and traditional tools can accelerate the refinement process:

- **Grammarly Premium** - Flags passive voice, wordiness, and tone inconsistencies.
- **Hemingway Editor** - Highlights long sentences, passive voice, and adverbs; gives a readability grade.
- **Paperpal** - Designed specifically for academic authors; it suggests formal alternatives and field-appropriate edits.
- **APA Style Blog Checklist** - Ensures consistency in terminology, citation formatting, and voice.

Always review AI suggestions critically—these tools are assistants, not authorities.

A Simple Step-by-Step Polishing Workflow

Here's a recommended daily checklist to apply across your literature review:

1. **Run a readability scan** using Hemingway or similar. Highlight sentences longer than 25 words for review.
2. **Read aloud** a page of your text and annotate any sentence that sounds unclear or stilted.
3. **Revise for voice** - Convert passive to active where possible.
4. **Cut filler** - Eliminate at least 10% of non-essential words from each paragraph.
5. **Improve transitions** - Add or revise connectors to improve paragraph cohesion.
6. **Check consistency** - Ensure consistent terminology, citation style, and verb tense throughout.
7. **Final digital sweep** - Run through Grammarly or Paperpal and apply useful suggestions.

Polishing in Action: A Before and After

Let's take a sample paragraph before revision:

"It has been found by researchers that students who use Instagram more than 3 hours a day tend to report higher anxiety levels. In a recent study, it was shown that students who engage more passively with content also experience more anxiety. These findings are important."

Now, revised with the principles above:

"Researchers have found that college students who use Instagram for more than three hours daily report higher levels of anxiety. Passive scrolling, in particular, appears linked to greater emotional distress (Smith, 2020). Together, these findings underscore the importance of examining how—and not just how much—students use social media."

Notice the active voice, sentence variety, improved transitions, and sharper focus.

The Scholarly Voice: Confidence Without Arrogance

Tone is the final polish. Graduate-level writing should project confidence in your analysis and care in your argumentation. Avoid hedging too much ("it seems," "perhaps," "one might say") unless the evidence is genuinely ambiguous. At the same time, steer clear of overstatements or sweeping claims. You are guiding the reader through complexity with clarity and poise.

Final Thoughts

Today's chapter marks a shift in your workflow: from construction to refinement, from structure to style. The ability to write clearly, elegantly, and persuasively is not an ornament—it is the medium of thought in academic life.

Next, in Day 21, you'll begin proofreading your full draft with fresh eyes, ready to finalize it for feedback, submission, or publication. For now, take pride in your voice. You've not only built something worth reading—you're making it a pleasure to read.

Next Steps

- Choose one section of your literature review and read it aloud. Annotate any sentence that sounds awkward or repetitive.
- Use your editing tool of choice (Grammarly, Hemingway, Paperpal) to flag complex or unclear phrasing. Apply changes judiciously.
- Revise your transitions to ensure smooth flow between ideas and sections.
- Create a "style snapshot": check for consistent voice, verb tense, citation terminology, and academic tone.
- Trim wordy paragraphs for conciseness—aim for clarity without sacrificing nuance.

Your review is no longer just a document—it is becoming a contribution.

Day 20 Summary Box

- Today's focus is on elevating your draft from **technically correct** to **professionally compelling**, refining style, tone, and paragraph flow.
- Good academic style is **clear, concise, and varied**—it earns trust and improves readability, citation potential, and review outcomes.
- Apply five core strategies:
  - **Read aloud** to spot awkward phrasing.
  - **Use active voice** to clarify agency.
  - **Vary sentence length** for rhythm and energy.
  - **Trim filler words** to strengthen clarity.
  - **Add precise transitions** to guide the reader through your logic.
- Use tools like **Grammarly**, **Hemingway**, and **Paperpal** to flag weak constructions, but **always apply human judgment** to revisions.
- Tone matters—project **confidence without arrogance** and balance precision with readability.

Day 21: Self-Editing Techniques

From First Draft to Final Polish: Becoming Your Own Best Editor

By Day 21, you've shaped your literature review into a complete chapter—introduction, thematic sections, debates, citations, and conclusion. But before it's truly ready for submission or feedback, it needs one more transformation: not of content, but of *refinement.* Today, you shift roles—from writer to editor—and apply a professional, methodical approach to self-editing that ensures your chapter is coherent, complete, and a pleasure to read.

Good editing is more than proofreading. It's about clarifying your logic, verifying structure, aligning tone, and catching the small (but cumulative) errors that undermine quality. It's about ensuring every idea is expressed as clearly and powerfully as possible—and that nothing distracts the reader from your argument.

Why Self-Editing Deserves a Full Day

Editing your own writing is hard. You know what you meant to say, which makes it easy to skim over missing links or vague phrases. That's why distance is your friend. Even a 24-hour break can help you see problems in structure, clarity, or citation you didn't notice during drafting.

It also matters because no one else will bring your level of insight to the review process—at least not yet. Before you hand your chapter over for supervisor or peer feedback, a careful internal audit sets the stage for more constructive critique later.

A Three-Pass Editing Framework

To avoid overwhelm and ensure thoroughness, this chapter introduces a three-pass system: macro, meso, and micro. Each pass focuses on a different level of your text, from structure down to style.

Macro Pass: Structure and Logic

This first sweep asks: *Is everything where it should be?* It's the most strategic layer of editing and the one that guards against the biggest issues—like missing themes, duplicated arguments, or disconnected sections.

- **Reverse Outline**: Take a blank page and write a one-sentence summary of each paragraph's main idea in order. Does each paragraph have a purpose? Do they flow logically? If you see repetition or a missing bridge between ideas, now's the time to revise.
- **Checklist Audit**: Use a structured checklist to confirm every core component is present and complete:
    - Introduction with context and purpose
    - 3–5 thematic sections, each with topic sentences, evidence, and transitions
    - Contradictions and debates discussed
    - Literature gap restated
    - Conclusion summarizing findings and leading into your study
    - All claims supported by citations
- **Heading Consistency**: Verify that all headings follow the same formatting (e.g., bold, sentence case, 14pt font). APA Style, for example, recommends bold, centered headings for top-level sections.

Meso Pass: Paragraph Flow and Transitions

Now, zoom in one level. Focus on how well each paragraph *functions* and connects with its neighbors.

- **Paragraph Check**: Each paragraph should contain a single clear idea, begin with a topic sentence, develop that idea with evidence or reasoning, and end with a linking or transition sentence.
- **Transition Audit**: Scan the ends and beginnings of paragraphs. Do they guide the reader from one idea to the next? Insert or revise transitions like:
    - *Moreover, Conversely, In contrast, For example, As a result*

When done right, transitions eliminate the need for signposting like "This paragraph will now..."—the logic becomes self-evident.

Micro Pass: Grammar, Style, and Readability

Finally, dig into the fine-grain edits. This is where your writing shifts from *competent* to *compelling.*

- **Read Aloud**: Hearing your work forces you to slow down and catch awkward phrasing or missing words. You can also use text-to-speech tools if you prefer not to read aloud yourself.
- **Readability Checks**: Paste your section into the Hemingway Editor to detect:
    - Sentences marked "very hard to read" (often >25 words)
    - Passive constructions
    - Overuse of adverbs or qualifiers
    - Opportunities for simplification
- **Grammar and Voice**: Use Grammarly or Paperpal to catch spelling, punctuation, and tone issues. Don't blindly accept changes—these tools are helpful but not infallible, especially in technical writing.
- **Citation Integrity**: Use Zotero's "Uncited Items" view or review your citation plugin's bibliography list. Ensure every in-text citation is matched with a full reference and vice versa. Eliminate duplicates, fix missing metadata (author names, years), and standardize formatting.

A Sample Editing Session in Practice

Let's say you're reviewing the section on "Social Media Usage and Anxiety." Here's what you might find during each pass:

- **Macro**: Two paragraphs cover similar findings—one from Facebook studies, one from Instagram. You decide to combine them into a broader "usage patterns" subtheme.
- **Meso**: You realize the first paragraph ends abruptly. You add: "These patterns set the stage for understanding how different platforms may influence mental health outcomes."
- **Micro**: Hemingway flags this sentence: "It has been noted by many researchers that the use of social media in an excessive way may possibly lead to increased anxiety symptoms." You revise it to: "Many researchers suggest that excessive social media use contributes to higher anxiety."

In 30 minutes, the section becomes more concise, coherent, and engaging.

Tool-Assisted Editing: What Works and When

Need	Tool	Use Tip
Distance from your draft	Pomofocus, Timer apps	Take a break: 25-minute edit blocks + 5-minute rest (Pomodoro method)
Reverse outline	Word comments or sticky notes	Write each paragraph's main idea in the margin
Style and readability check	Hemingway Editor	Highlight long/complex sentences and passive voice
Grammar and tone check	Grammarly / Paperpal	Use for polish, not for deep revision
Citation consistency	Zotero plugin	"Add/Edit Bibliography" → live reference list
Heading audit	APA Formatting Guide	Download APA's PDF checklist for formatting and headings

Final Editing Checklist

Before you call this chapter finished, walk through these final checks:

- All required sections are present and logically ordered.
- Every paragraph has a topic sentence and a summarizing or linking line.
- Transitions guide the reader from one idea to the next.
- Readability is strong: no sentences marked "very hard," minimal passive voice.
- Citations are accurate, complete, and match your reference list.
- Headings follow a consistent and appropriate style.
- Tone is confident, scholarly, and respectful of complexity.

Reflection: From Rough Draft to Reader-Ready

Self-editing isn't just about catching mistakes—it's about honoring your ideas. When you take time to polish your work, you show your reader (and yourself) that your insights matter enough to be delivered well.

By now, your literature review is no longer a raw collection of summaries and citations. It is a shaped, structured, and stylistically sound argument—clear in purpose, rich in evidence, and professional in tone.

Next, in Day 22, you'll step into the phase: seeking and integrating external feedback. But for today, enjoy the quiet satisfaction of improving your own work. It's one of the most empowering skills any scholar can cultivate.

Next Steps

- Schedule your macro/meso/micro editing passes with breaks in between.
- Run your draft through readability and citation tools.
- Highlight any uncertain or awkward sections for peer or supervisor review.
- Save a version with tracked changes or annotations to document your edits.

You've moved from idea to draft to polished manuscript—and you did it one deliberate day at a time.

Day 21 Summary Box

- Today, you shift from **writer to editor**, using a structured three-pass framework—**macro, meso, and micro**—to refine your literature review.
- Self-editing enhances clarity, flow, and professionalism by revisiting structure, transitions, tone, and citation accuracy.
- Use a **macro pass** to audit chapter structure and logic, with a reverse outline and section checklist.
- Apply a **meso pass** to improve paragraph flow, transitions, and internal coherence.
- Conduct a **micro pass** to polish grammar, simplify language, improve readability, and align citation and heading formats.
- Tools like **Hemingway**, **Grammarly**, and **Zotero** support this process—but your judgment remains essential.

Day 22: Seeking and Incorporating Feedback

Turning Your Literature Review into a Stronger, Sharper Argument

You've written, edited, and polished your literature review chapter with great care. But now, on Day 22, you take one of the most vital steps in academic writing: inviting other eyes into your process. Feedback is not a threat to your voice—it's a lens through which you refine it.

Whether from a supervisor, a fellow graduate student, a writing center tutor, or an AI writing assistant, external input helps you see what your brain is trained to overlook: unclear logic, inconsistent tone, confusing phrasing, or unwarranted assumptions. And if approached strategically, feedback doesn't just fix surface flaws—it elevates the structure and argument of your chapter.

This chapter will walk you through how to seek feedback intentionally, how to interpret and categorize it, and how to decide what to change, what to question, and what to keep. By the end, your literature review won't just be "done"—it will be clearer, sharper, and more persuasive to readers beyond yourself.

Why Feedback Is Essential—Even for Skilled Writers

Research in writing pedagogy confirms what most of us know intuitively: we can't reliably evaluate our own clarity. The University of North Carolina's Writing Center notes that outside readers challenge the internal logic of your argument and force you to clarify what you assumed was obvious. Similarly, studies show that students who actively revise based on structured peer or supervisor feedback produce higher-quality, more publishable manuscripts than those who rely solely on self-editing.

Feedback helps you answer the ultimate reader's question: *Does this make sense to someone else?*

Step 1: Choose the Right Reviewers—and Frame Your Ask

Not all feedback is equal. A friend who's unfamiliar with academic writing may not be able to help with coherence or citation logic. Likewise, an advisor may give strategic guidance but not mark sentence-level issues. Think of feedback sources as specialists:

Reviewer Type	Strength	How to Frame Your Ask
Peer in your field	Knows your topic and jargon	Ask for comments on logic, clarity, and flow
Advisor or supervisor	Focuses on big-picture contributions	Send them your gap statement and research rationale
Writing tutor or editor	Assesses tone, clarity, and structure	Request help with transitions, paragraph flow, and style
AI assistant (e.g. ChatGPT)	Instant, non-judgmental, good for draft diagnostics	Use targeted prompts like: "Suggest improvements to flow and clarity in this paragraph."

Pro tip: When you send your draft, include 2–3 specific questions. For example:

- "Does Theme 2 flow logically into Theme 3?"
- "Are any sections too repetitive?"
- "Which part felt unclear or overly dense?"

A focused request makes it easier for your reviewer—and more useful for you.

Step 2: Use Collaborative Tools to Capture and Organize Feedback

Digital tools make the feedback process efficient and trackable. Google Docs, Microsoft Word, and Overleaf (for LaTeX users) all allow reviewers to leave in-line comments, suggest edits, or track changes.

- **Google Docs (Suggest Mode)**: Reviewers can propose edits you can approve or reject with one click.
- **Microsoft Word (Track Changes)**: Standard for academic collaboration; shows every addition, deletion, and comment.
- **Grammarly or Paperpal**: Use these for grammar and tone diagnostics—not as your only editor, but as a pre-pass before human feedback.

Once feedback arrives, don't dive in blindly. Start by reading all comments in one sitting without editing anything. Let them sink in. Then begin triaging.

Step 3: Triage, Log, and Act

Treat feedback like data. Organize it, evaluate it, then implement changes selectively.

Triage: Sort feedback into two categories:

- **Global**: Suggestions that affect argument structure, theme organization, or logic.
- **Local**: Edits related to grammar, word choice, sentence clarity, or citations.

Log: Use a simple feedback matrix to track responses:

Comment	Action Taken	Status
Paragraph 2 lacks a topic sentence	Added new lead-in clarifying its focus	☑ Done
Theme 3 transition felt abrupt	Inserted linking sentence between themes	☑ Done
Sentence in Section 4 unclear ("confusing")	Rewrote for clarity	✕ Recheck later

Act: Make changes that clearly improve logic or clarity. For ambiguous suggestions, ask clarifying questions or discuss them with your supervisor. For feedback you disagree with, be ready to justify your choice in a future draft or conversation.

Step 4: Using AI as a Feedback Partner (With Caution)

AI writing assistants can serve as useful first-pass reviewers, particularly when time is short. But they must be used critically and ethically.

Try prompting with:

"Act as a peer reviewer. Highlight one unclear sentence, one strong paragraph, and one idea that could benefit from more evidence."

Or:

"Suggest three ways to improve paragraph flow in the following excerpt."

Just remember: AI lacks domain expertise. You are the final authority. Never accept a suggested change that alters the intent or introduces inaccuracy.

Step 5: Revising with Confidence, Not Compromise

Not all feedback should be accepted. Your literature review reflects your scholarly voice, and you're allowed to disagree. But you must do so thoughtfully.

- **Accept suggestions that clarify your message.**
- **Reject suggestions that derail your focus—but log why.**
- **Adapt suggestions that point to a problem but propose the wrong fix.**

This approach not only improves your draft—it also models the professional peer-review process in academic publishing, where thoughtful response letters often matter as much as the revised manuscript.

Final Reflections: What Feedback Teaches You

Feedback isn't just about this chapter. It teaches you how others read your work, where your assumptions go unspoken, and how your argument lands with a fresh mind. Incorporating that input now prepares you for supervisor meetings, peer review, conference proposals, and beyond.

By seeing feedback not as correction but as collaboration, you grow as a scholar—and ensure your literature review lands with the clarity, credibility, and coherence it deserves.

Quick Summary: Feedback Integration Workflow

1. **Choose your reviewers** carefully—aim for diversity in perspectives.
2. **Frame your ask** clearly—give them questions, not just your file.
3. **Collect feedback** via collaborative platforms.
4. **Triage** feedback into global vs. local.
5. **Log and revise** using a simple feedback matrix.

6. **Document your decisions**—especially when you decline a change.
7. **Reflect on your process**—it builds long-term editorial resilience.

Next Steps

- Email or share your draft with two trusted reviewers.
- Begin populating your feedback matrix with their responses.
- Revise one global and three local elements from their suggestions.
- Prepare a short reflection on what surprised you about their comments.

Next, in Day 23, we'll turn to the finishing touches—proofreading, formatting, and final submission prep. But for now, congratulate yourself: you've opened your writing to dialogue, and that is the mark of a true scholar.

Day 22 Summary Box

- Today's focus is on **transforming your polished draft** into a stronger, clearer, and more persuasive chapter through strategic feedback.
- Feedback is essential—not just for fixing grammar, but for **clarifying logic, strengthening structure**, and exposing assumptions you may not see yourself.
- Choose reviewers intentionally—supervisors for big-picture thinking, peers for clarity and flow, writing tutors for structure and style, and AI tools for fast diagnostics.
- Frame your request with **2–3 targeted questions** to get actionable, relevant feedback.
- Use **Google Docs, Word Track Changes**, or Overleaf for efficient, trackable collaboration.
- Triage responses into **global (structural)** vs. **local (sentence-level)** edits, and log changes using a **feedback matrix**.
- Accept helpful revisions, question unclear ones, and confidently decline suggestions that don't align with your vision—just be ready to explain why.

Day 23: Revising and Refining Your Draft

By this point in your literature review journey, you've written your full chapter, sought feedback, and made preliminary edits. But a strong draft is not yet a polished chapter. Day 23 is your invitation to shift from editing what's there to strategically refining the entire piece—revisiting structure, improving paragraph cohesion, tightening your prose, and ensuring that your argument holds together seamlessly. This isn't about correcting typos. It's about elevating your text from "finished" to *publishable*.

This chapter offers a layered revision framework, moving from structural logic to paragraph transitions and finally to sentence-level clarity. As with any academic writing, your goal is not just accuracy—it's clarity, cohesion, and rhetorical power.

Why Deep Revision Still Matters

Even after multiple rounds of writing and feedback, inconsistencies often remain. A new paragraph might disrupt the flow of an earlier section. A quote added to clarify may make a previous explanation redundant. And revisions made in response to feedback might unintentionally introduce new gaps.

More importantly, this is the moment to reclaim ownership of your argument. Feedback helps shape the review, but your voice must tie it all together. Day 23 helps you refine and unify that voice across the entire chapter.

Step 1: The Global (Macro) Pass

Revisiting structure and overall logic

Create a Reverse Outline

Print or open your draft and write a two- to five-word summary in the margin of every paragraph. This simple step—known as reverse outlining—instantly reveals weak spots:

- Do any two paragraphs say essentially the same thing?
- Is there a gap where a new idea should be introduced?
- Do the headings still reflect the content beneath them?

You may find a theme that has grown too long and needs splitting or, conversely, a section that seems underdeveloped. This reverse outline is your structural X-ray.

Review Your Feedback Matrix

Revisit the feedback you received on Day 22 and your responses. Sort comments into three actionable types:

- **Add Evidence** - Have you supported each major claim with sufficient studies?
- **Clarify Logic** - Do transitions or framing sentences guide the reader?
- **Trim/Move Content** - Have redundant or disjointed ideas been addressed?

Now's the time to implement the final high-impact revisions that strengthen your argument without bloating it.

Align Your Headings with the Original Outline

Compare each heading in your chapter with the structured outline you finalized around Day 12. Ensure they still reflect the content below. If a heading has changed in tone or topic, update it accordingly. In APA style, level 2 headings should be bold, title case, and flush left. Keep formatting consistent.

Step 2: The Paragraph-Level (Meso) Pass

Ensuring flow, clarity, and balance

Strengthen Transitions

Every paragraph should connect logically to what comes before and signal what's next. Read the first and last sentence of each paragraph. Do they help your reader transition smoothly?

If not, insert or revise linking phrases such as:

- "Building on previous findings..."
- "In contrast to earlier results..."
- "This leads to the next consideration..."

These transition phrases are not just stylistic—they support argument coherence and reader comprehension.

Check Paragraph Cohesion and Length

Each paragraph should cover one idea only, supported by 2–4 pieces of evidence or explanation. If a paragraph feels too long (over 200 words) or contains multiple points, split it. If a paragraph feels too thin, enrich it with examples, a summary sentence, or a cross-study comparison.

Step 3: The Sentence-Level (Micro) Pass

Polishing expression, tone, and style

Read Aloud or Use Text-to-Speech

Reading aloud activates different areas of the brain than silent reading. You'll catch missing words, awkward phrasing, and unnatural transitions. Many writers report catching double the number of issues this way.

Active Voice and Concision

Use active constructions wherever clarity allows. Instead of:

"It was found that students using Instagram experienced more anxiety," try:
"Students using Instagram reported higher anxiety levels."

Also remove filler words like "very," "actually," "really," and "in order to"—unless they add precise meaning.

Consistency Audit

Choose one tense (present or past) and one voice (first-person singular or impersonal) and apply it uniformly. Ensure terms like "Instagram," "social media platforms," or acronyms are used consistently throughout. Confirm that your in-text citations follow the same format (e.g., Smith, 2020).

Step 4: Final Check—References, Headings, and Tables

- Use your reference manager (Zotero, EndNote, etc.) to generate and update your bibliography.
- Check that every in-text citation corresponds to a full reference entry.
- Verify that any tables or figures have:
    - A number (Table 1, Table 2...)
    - A descriptive title in title case
    - A mention in the main text (e.g., "See Table 1").

If you made any new additions to support feedback revisions, regenerate the bibliography to reflect these changes.

Support Tools to Streamline the Process

Need	Tool	How It Helps
Reverse outlining	Google Docs Outline Pane	Navigate headers and subheaders quickly.
Flow & transitions	UNC Transition Guide	Provides connectors and examples for smooth linkage.
Readability check	Hemingway App	Highlights sentence complexity and adverb overload.
Citation refresh	Zotero Refresh Button	Updates bibliography with all recent changes.

Final Tips

- Don't revise blindly—check each edit improves clarity, coherence, or precision.
- If you rewrote any sections, re-read surrounding paragraphs to ensure the new content fits seamlessly.
- Your tone should now feel scholarly, your arguments complete, and your transitions organic.

Your Chapter, Now a Scholarly Contribution

After this full-body revision, your literature review chapter should read not as a series of assembled parts but as a cohesive academic narrative. It will present a clear line of argument, supported by well-integrated sources, with a consistent style and professional polish.

This version is not only readable—it's submission-ready.

Summary: Revision Checklist

Stage	Key Task	☑
Global Pass	Reverse outline, fix structure, confirm all themes	
Paragraph Flow	Add transitions, check idea focus, trim or expand	
Sentence Polish	Read aloud, revise for clarity and conciseness	
Consistency Pass	Tense, terminology, headings, and citation style	
Final Reference	Refresh bibliography, check table labels and captions	

Next Steps

- Complete your revision log noting the most impactful change you made.
- Prepare your draft for final proofing and formatting on Day 24.
- If desired, submit to a writing center or mentor for a final quality check.

You've revised not just a document, but your argument and voice as a researcher. Congratulations—the hard craft is nearly complete.

Day 23 Summary Box

- Today's focus is **deep revision**—moving beyond fixing sentences to reshaping structure, improving cohesion, and refining your academic voice.
- Begin with a **macro-level pass**: use reverse outlining to identify gaps, redundancies, and misaligned sections. Ensure your headings match your original outline and reflect current content.
- Use your **feedback matrix** from Day 22 to implement targeted improvements in logic, evidence, and organization.
- Conduct a **paragraph-level pass**: strengthen transitions, split long paragraphs, and ensure each section flows logically and smoothly.
- Follow with a **micro-level polish**: revise for clarity, eliminate filler, favor active voice, and ensure consistent terminology and citation style.
- Update all references and regenerate your bibliography with Zotero or your preferred manager. Review tables, headings, and labels for formatting compliance.

Day 24: Proofreading for Grammar and Clarity

After days of building a coherent narrative, integrating sources, responding to feedback, and revising each section for clarity and flow, your literature review chapter is now structurally solid and intellectually sound. What remains is a final, careful pass: a meticulous proofreading round that catches every comma splice, misplaced article, and inconsistent heading—small errors that, if left unattended, can undercut the professionalism of your work.

Day 24 is not about rewriting. It is about refining. This is the moment to polish your writing so that your argument shines without distraction. Readers—especially supervisors, reviewers, or committee members—should focus on your insight, not stumble over typos or formatting flaws.

Why Proofreading Deserves Its Own Day

Studies in editing and cognitive psychology have repeatedly shown that surface errors affect credibility. Misspellings, grammatical slips, or inconsistent formatting—even if minor—create friction for the reader. Worse, they signal haste or inattention. A polished manuscript, by contrast, reinforces your authority as a researcher and your respect for academic standards.

Proofreading also involves a different mindset than revision. Revision asks "What am I trying to say?" Proofreading asks "Am I saying it clearly, correctly, and consistently?"

The Three-Part Proofreading Method

Reset Your Attention

Before diving in, step away. Even a short 24-hour break improves your ability to spot mistakes. This "attention reset" reduces the chance your brain will auto-correct errors during re-reading. If you've been staring at this chapter for days, distance is your ally.

Deploy a Structured Proofreading Routine

Read Aloud

Whether you read to yourself, a peer, or use text-to-speech software, hearing your writing exposes awkward phrases, missing transitions, and stilted rhythm. The human ear is a powerful editor.

Example: You might catch a phrase like, *"The researchers were found to have conducted..."* and revise to *"The researchers conducted..."*

Read Backwards

Starting from the final sentence and moving upward, sentence by sentence, allows you to focus on grammar and punctuation out of narrative context. This is especially useful for spotting:

- Missed articles ("the" vs. "a")
- Homophones (their/there/they're; it's/its)
- Extra or missing commas and periods

Use Digital Tools—But Not Blindly

Run your document through a spelling and grammar checker such as:

- **Word or Google Docs spellcheck** (good for basic typos)
- **Grammarly or Paperpal** (flags passive voice, comma splices, article usage)

Important: Always verify before accepting suggestions. Grammar checkers can misunderstand academic phrasing or "correct" technical terms.

Common Grammar and Style Errors to Check

Issue	Check Example
Subject–verb agreement	*"The results shows" → "The results show"*
Comma splice	*"The data was clear, it was ignored." → use semicolon or separate.*
Homophones	*"Effect" vs "Affect"
Article use	*"A analysis" → "An analysis"*
Unnecessary modifiers	Remove "very," "really," "actually" if they add no meaning

3. Conduct a Formatting Consistency Audit

Once grammar is clean, switch focus to the visual presentation. Inconsistencies here can make even strong writing look sloppy.

Headings

- **APA Style:** Use boldface and title case (e.g., "Social Media and Mental Health")
- Ensure heading levels are used consistently throughout (no jumps from Level 1 to Level 3)

Font and Spacing

- Same font throughout the document (usually 12pt Times New Roman or as required)
- Double spacing unless specified otherwise
- Indents applied consistently to all paragraphs

Reference List

- Use your reference manager (e.g., Zotero) to regenerate the list
- Check for:
    - **Hanging indents**

- **Correct punctuation in citations**
- **Alphabetical ordering**
- **One-to-one match** between in-text and reference list entries

APA tip: In APA 7, periods and commas usually go *inside* quotation marks, unless the punctuation is not part of the quote.

Support Tools for Final Proofreading

Tool	Purpose
Grammarly	Grammar, sentence structure, article use
Hemingway App	Readability check (long sentences, passive voice)
Google Docs / Word	Track changes, comments, spellcheck
Zotero "Refresh"	Updates bibliography with latest citations
Text-to-Speech	Auditory proofing of long passages

Final Proofreading Checklist

Task	☑
Spellcheck run and all suggestions reviewed	
Grammar check: subject–verb, comma use, etc.	
Homophones and confusing word pairs verified	
All headings use correct APA level and format	
Font, spacing, and indentation are consistent	
Reference list has no duplicates or errors	
Each in-text citation matches a full reference	
Quotes include page numbers if required	

Bringing It All Together

You've now moved from raw notes and fragmented studies to a clear, scholarly narrative—fully supported by evidence, reviewed by peers, and refined for readability. Proofreading is your final quality check before submission.

Even a beautifully argued chapter can be marred by distracting errors. But with today's thorough proofing—backed by smart tools, attentive reading, and formatting vigilance—you have ensured your ideas will be heard clearly and respectfully.

What's Next?

Next, in Day 25, you will take the final step: preparing your literature review for formal submission, publication, or presentation. That means file format checks, cover page details, metadata, and version control.

Today, celebrate. Your chapter is not just finished—it's polished.

Reflection Prompt (Optional)

Write a short paragraph (50–75 words) noting one recurring writing mistake you caught during proofreading, and how you now spot and fix it.

Next Steps

- Complete any final citations, tables, or figures
- Save your clean copy in multiple formats (.docx, .pdf)
- Begin Day 25 with a full backup and submission prep checklist

Your literature review is now a professional-grade academic artifact—clear, cohesive, and publication-ready.

Day 24 Summary Box

- Today's focus is **precision and polish**—refining grammar, punctuation, style, and formatting to ensure your literature review is clear, credible, and distraction-free.
- Use a **three-part proofreading method**:
    - Read aloud to catch awkward phrasing.
    - Read backwards to focus on grammar and surface-level issues.
    - Use tools like Grammarly or Hemingway—but always review their suggestions critically.
- Watch for **common grammar errors**: subject–verb agreement, article use, comma splices, and wordy modifiers.
- Audit your **formatting**: APA heading levels, consistent fonts, double spacing, proper indentation, and a clean, alphabetized reference list with no missing or duplicate entries.
- Use your reference manager (e.g., Zotero) to **refresh your bibliography** and confirm all in-text citations match reference entries.

Day 25: Formatting References and Final Touches

After weeks of critical reading, detailed synthesis, structured writing, and deliberate revision, you've reached the final stretch: formatting and finishing. On Day 25, your goal is simple—but significant. You're not adding new content, but ensuring that your literature review chapter *looks* as strong as it reads. Style consistency, reference precision, and clean document layout all signal academic excellence. These finishing details separate a good draft from a submission-ready manuscript.

By the end of this chapter, your literature review should meet professional standards in every aspect: citation formatting, caption clarity, layout alignment, and template compliance. This is the last check before you print, submit, or share—so let's get it right.

Why Formatting Matters

Formatting is more than cosmetic. Readers—especially supervisors and examiners—often form their first impression not from your argument, but from your presentation. Sloppy references, misaligned headings, and inconsistent spacing suggest haste or carelessness, even when the content is solid. But a well-formatted manuscript tells the opposite story: that you are precise, methodical, and serious about your scholarly craft.

Moreover, formatting errors are often what examiners *do* comment on, even when they're otherwise impressed with your writing. Fortunately, formatting perfection is a task you can control entirely—and Day 25 shows you how.

Step 1: Perfecting the Reference List

Reference accuracy is non-negotiable. Each in-text citation must match a reference entry—and every reference must be cleanly formatted, free of duplicates, and styled consistently.

Task	Rule or Standard
Hanging indents	First line flush left, rest indented 0.5" (APA 7 §9.44)
Journal titles italicized	APA & MLA require this; article titles in sentence case
Alphabetical order	Sort by first author surname (APA, MLA)
Consistent punctuation	Use periods and commas per your style guide
No orphaned or ghost citations	Every in-text citation must appear in the reference list

Quick Tip: Run a search for *et al.*—if that author group isn't matched in your reference list, you've got a ghost citation to fix.

Tools to Use:

- **Zotero's "Duplicate Items" tab** to merge near-identical entries
- **ReciteWorks** to automatically detect citation-reference mismatches
- **Manual scan** for hanging indents and italics

Step 2: Reviewing Figures, Tables, and Appendices

If your chapter includes tables or figures, Day 25 is when you make them visually and structurally consistent.

Formatting Rules for Visual Elements (APA 7)

- **Figures**: Caption appears *below* the figure (e.g., *Figure 1. Distribution of Themes in Reviewed Literature*)
- **Tables**: Caption appears *above*
- **Numbering**: Number consecutively in order of appearance
- **Referencing**: Every figure/table must be cited at least once in the main text

- **Appendices**: Label as *Appendix A*, *Appendix B*, etc., and refer to them clearly in the body

Ensure alignment, font sizing, and line spacing are also uniform across all visual materials.

Step 3: Running a Full Formatting Audit

Now, scroll from the top of your document to the bottom and check that every element follows your department or journal's required formatting style.

Element	What to Check
Title page	Is it styled per institutional requirements?
Chapter title	Example: *Chapter 2: Literature Review* – bold, centered, title case
Headings	Use consistent level styles (APA: bold, title case)
Font and spacing	Same font and size throughout; double-spaced text
Page numbers	Usually bottom center or top right—check template
Running head	APA Student Paper: no running head unless required
Margins	Standard 1" on all sides unless specified otherwise
Table of contents (if required)	Ensure page numbers match your chapter layout

Finally, export to PDF to check that formatting remains intact and nothing shifts unexpectedly between platforms.

Step 4: Style Guide Swap (If Required)

If your chapter will eventually be published or submitted to a journal with a different reference style (e.g., from APA to Chicago or IEEE), use your reference manager (e.g., Zotero or Mendeley) to instantly reformat your citations by switching the CSL (Citation Style Language) file.

Reminder: This only works if your citations are still live (not converted to plain text). Avoid manually editing citations until the very end.

Step 5: One-Hour Final Touches Workflow

Set aside one dedicated hour to walk through this final checklist.

1. **Zotero Refresh** – Sync citations and rebuild bibliography.
2. **ReciteWorks Check** – Resolve flagged mismatches or missing references.
3. **Figure/Table Audit** – Scroll through all captions and verify in-text mentions.
4. **Reference List Scan** – Confirm italics, punctuation, and alphabetisation.
5. **PDF Export** – Print to PDF and scroll through to verify layout and spacing.
6. **One Last Read** – Skim top to bottom. Catch any spacing oddities, stray italics, or leftover highlight marks.

Celebrate the Finish

Today marks a significant milestone. You've taken your literature review from rough outline to research-grade chapter—rigorously argued, properly referenced, and polished for professional presentation.

Next Days's Preview

On Day 26, we'll take a step back and reflect on what you've accomplished—and outline next steps in your thesis journey. Whether you're moving into your methodology chapter, preparing for submission, or presenting your findings, you'll now have the foundation of a well-crafted review to build upon.

Final Sprint Task for Day 25: "Finish Line Audit"

Step	Task	Evidence
1. Reference perfection	Hanging indents, italics, proper punctuation	*LitReview_Refs_FINAL.docx*
2. Cross-check citations	Pick 3 in-text citations and 3 reference entries to verify matches	Checklist screenshot
3. Visual consistency check	Tables/figures numbered, captioned, and cited in-text	Annotated PDF with comments
4. Apply formatting template	Page numbers, margins, font, title formatting	*LitReview_Final.pdf*
5. Final read-through	Note two small fixes still made (spacing, italics)	50-word reflection journal

Reflection Prompt (Optional)

What small formatting error took longer than expected to fix today, and how will you prevent it in future chapters?

You've done it. Your literature review is now a clean, compelling, and professionally formatted piece of academic work—ready to be shared, submitted, or celebrated.

With your literature review now written, cited, and polished, you've crossed a major threshold in your dissertation journey. But your work doesn't end here. In the next phase, we'll explore how your literature review connects directly to your research methods—bridging what's known with what you plan to investigate. These final days of the sprint focus on continuity, coherence, and preparing for what comes next. Your chapter is ready—but your thesis is still unfolding.

Day 25 Summary Box

- Today's focus is on **presentation perfection**: finalizing references, formatting figures and tables, and aligning your document with academic style standards.
- Use **Zotero or your reference manager** to ensure all in-text citations match the bibliography, are alphabetized, and use hanging indents, italics, and correct punctuation (APA, MLA, or other).
- Review and refine **tables and figures**: number sequentially, format captions (above for tables, below for figures), and confirm in-text mentions.
- Conduct a **document-wide formatting audit**: headings, font, spacing, page numbers, and margins should follow institutional or journal guidelines.
- Export your chapter as a PDF and perform a **top-to-bottom visual check** to catch any layout issues, broken citations, or leftover edits.

PART V: TRANSITION AND REFLECT

Day 26: Linking to Research Methods

Now that your literature review chapter is nearly complete—evidence synthesized, gaps identified, and arguments polished—it's time to connect your findings to the next stage of your thesis: the research methodology. Chapter 26 focuses on building that vital intellectual bridge. This bridge isn't always written explicitly into the literature review chapter itself (unless your supervisor prefers it), but it should always be conceptualized and sketched in your notes. By crafting a clear, logical connection between what the literature lacks and how your study intends to address that absence, you ensure the coherence and legitimacy of your research design.

Why This Transition Matters

The best literature reviews do more than summarize previous studies—they lay the groundwork for original inquiry. As methodological scholars like Creswell emphasize, the link between your literature review and research design must be *intentional and aligned.* If your review reveals that most studies on social media and anxiety ignore platform-specific effects or fail to explore non-Western populations, your method should clearly respond to that.

Examiners often describe this continuity as the "golden thread"—a visible line that runs from your review to your research questions and into your design. When this thread is clear, your entire thesis gains cohesion, credibility, and rigor.

Step 1: Reaffirm the Gap

Return to the gap you articulated earlier (likely on Day 11). Write it again in slightly refined form, integrating any new clarity you've gained since completing the chapter.

Example:
"Despite extensive research on social media and mental health, few studies have examined platform-specific effects—particularly those of TikTok—on anxiety among students in United States."

Maintain consistency of phrasing with your earlier gap statement. This will later help you echo that gap in both your research question and design justification.

Step 2: Match the Method to the Gap

Your gap will naturally suggest the type of method needed to explore it.

Gap Type	Appropriate Method
Lack of platform-level comparison	Cross-sectional survey or platform usage logs
No longitudinal data on anxiety trajectories	Panel design or diary method
Missing non-Western perspectives	Culturally adapted instruments; regional sampling
Conflicting findings on content types	Mixed methods (e.g., content analysis + interviews)
Little knowledge of subjective experiences	Qualitative interviews or thematic analysis

The goal is *fit*. A good research design doesn't just look rigorous—it directly addresses the limitations uncovered in the literature.

Step 3: Write the Bridge Paragraph

Now draft a three-sentence transition that conceptually links your literature review to your forthcoming methods chapter. This paragraph may appear at the end of your literature review or the beginning of Chapter 3 (depending on your institutional style), but it will always serve the same function.

Bridge Paragraph Template:

1. *Lead-in*: Summarize what the literature shows.
2. *Gap reiteration*: Reassert what's missing.
3. *Methodological rationale*: Briefly state what design you'll use and why.

Example:
"The preceding review highlights the growing concern around social media's psychological effects, particularly anxiety. However, little research has examined how TikTok's algorithm-driven content affects student mental health in non-Western contexts. To address this gap, this study employs a longitudinal survey design that tracks daily TikTok use and self-reported anxiety among Emirati undergraduates over an academic term."

This paragraph ensures your reader knows *why* your study exists and *why* your chosen method is the right response.

Step 4: Build a Gap–Method Matrix

To clarify alignment even further, create a simple table that matches the gaps you've identified to the specific methods or variables you'll employ.

Gap	Methodological Response	Target Variable/Outcome
No data on TikTok in The United States	Cross-sectional student survey	Daily TikTok use + GAD-7 anxiety
Lack of time-sensitive data	6-week panel study	Anxiety change over time
Platform comparison missing	Multi-platform usage questionnaire	Comparative effect by platform

This matrix can be pasted into your research notebook or your methodology draft. It will help you explain your design choices clearly and defend them during proposal presentations or vivas.

Step 5: Store and Prepare for Chapter 3

Save your bridge paragraph, gap re-statement, and gap-method matrix under your **Chapter 3** folder or section header. When you begin writing your methodology chapter, these elements will become the backbone of your *design rationale*—and save you hours of backtracking.

Quick Save Tip:

Label this note file as: `Ch3_intro_scaffold.md`

Common Pitfalls—and How to Avoid Them

Pitfall	How to Fix It
Method doesn't actually address the gap	Re-read your gap and research questions before finalizing design
Over-scoping the design	Focus on one primary gap; list others as future work
Vague phrasing ("explore," "examine")	Use stronger verbs: "measure," "model," "compare," "test"

Today's Sprint Task: Designing the Bridge

Task	Output
Restate your main gap	2–3 sentence text block
Write a bridge paragraph	Use the three-sentence template
Draft a gap-method matrix	Table linking gap → method → variable
Share the bridge paragraph with a peer	Ask: "Does this method clearly address the gap?"
Save outputs under Chapter 3 folder	Label: Methodology_Intro_Bridge.docx

Reflection Prompt

What specific feature of your design most clearly addresses the literature gap you identified? Could an examiner trace your reasoning back through the review and say, "Yes, this method fits"?

Next Steps

Next, in Day 27, we'll turn the focus from structure to self: how you, the researcher, managed the process, grew through the challenge, and are preparing for what's next. Day 27 is your moment to pause, reflect, and recognize your academic evolution.

Your literature review is no longer an isolated chapter—it's a launchpad for your study. Well done.

Day 26 Summary Box

- Today's focus is on conceptually connecting your **literature review** to your **research methodology**—ensuring your design directly addresses the gap you identified.
- Revisit your **refined gap statement** and align it with an appropriate method (e.g., survey, longitudinal, qualitative) that logically responds to what's missing in the literature.
- Draft a **bridge paragraph** (3 sentences) that transitions from your review to your methods: summarize the literature, reiterate the gap, and justify your chosen design.
- Build a **Gap-Method Matrix** to clearly link each identified gap to a specific methodological response and measurable variable or outcome.
- Save these elements in your methodology folder (e.g., Methodology_Intro_Bridge.docx) for easy reference as you begin Chapter 3.

Day 27: Planning the Methodology Chapter

As you close the final pages of your literature review chapter, Day 27 asks you to shift your perspective: from interpreting what's known to planning how to discover what's not. This transition—from reader to researcher, from critic to creator—is more than academic protocol. It's a philosophical pivot. You now possess a detailed understanding of your research landscape, including what's been studied, what hasn't, and why it matters. Your next move is to define how *you* will fill that gap.

The goal of this chapter is not to write your methodology yet—but to construct a clear, defensible, and feasible outline of your research design. Think of it as assembling the scaffolding before building the walls. Done right, it becomes the blueprint that will carry you seamlessly into Chapter 3.

Why You Should Plan Before You Write

Too many methodology chapters falter not because the research is flawed, but because the plan was never clear. Students dive into procedural detail without connecting it to the literature review, or they improvise design choices without considering feasibility. Research design scholar John Creswell reminds us that methodological alignment is the "bedrock of research validity." Planning, then, is not just about efficiency—it's about credibility.

In fact, studies show that students who draft their methodology skeletons *before* writing experience fewer supervisor revisions, complete their theses more quickly, and gain faster ethics approval.

Step 1: Anchor to the Research Question and Gap

Begin with the essentials: write your research question at the top of your draft, followed by the three-sentence bridge paragraph you crafted on Day 26. These two pieces will keep your design aligned and defensible.

Example Research Question

How does daily TikTok use predict anxiety trajectories among first-year Emirati students?

Bridge Paragraph

Prior research has shown conflicting evidence on social media's impact on student anxiety, particularly for image- and video-based platforms. However, no studies to date have explored TikTok use in American student populations over time. To address this gap, the present study employs a two-wave longitudinal survey to examine the association between daily TikTok usage and anxiety levels across a semester.

This single pairing grounds every decision that follows.

Step 2: Outline Core Design Elements

Now identify each component of your study. At this stage, it doesn't have to be prose—just a well-structured outline will do. Include the following elements:

Participants & Sampling

- **Target Sample**: 200 first-year undergraduates from UAE universities.
- **Inclusion Criteria**: Aged 18–24, enrolled full-time, use TikTok ≥3x per week.
- **Sampling Technique**: Stratified convenience sample via university mailing lists.

Use tools like CloudResearch's sample size calculator to justify numbers based on power analysis (e.g., 95% power, medium effect size = ~197 participants).

Instruments

- **Anxiety**: GAD-7 (Generalized Anxiety Disorder scale) – reliable, validated, used in student populations.
- **Social Media Use**: Custom frequency questionnaire (hours/day per platform).
- **Demographics**: Age, gender, field of study, prior mental health diagnosis.

Ensure each scale has documented reliability (α ≥ 0.80) from prior literature or pilot data.

Procedures

- **Data Collection**: Two-wave online survey via Qualtrics; 6-week interval.
- **Recruitment**: Email invitation + reminders at Week 2 and Week 5.
- **Consent**: Online form at start of survey; IRB-approved script.

Data Analysis

- **Plan**: Multiple regression with anxiety as DV; TikTok hours as IV; control for gender and prior anxiety history.
- **Optional Extension**: Change score analysis across waves (Wave 2 – Wave 1 anxiety).

Step 3: Plan for Practical Implementation

Even the most elegant design is useless without logistical planning.

Ethics & IRB

- **Approval Type**: Likely exempt or expedited; prepare protocol and instruments.
- **Lead Time**: Allow 4–6 weeks for review and revision (check your institution's IRB calendar).
- **Social Media Ethics**: Follow best practices for digital privacy (e.g., no screen scraping, explicit consent for usage reporting).

Pilot Testing

- **Pilot Group**: 10 students from similar demographic.
- **Goal**: Test clarity of items, estimate completion time, compute Cronbach's α for GAD-7 in your sample.

Timeline

Create a Gantt-style timeline with monthly goals:

Month	Activity
M1	Finalize design, prep IRB
M2	IRB review and feedback
M3	Pilot study, instrument tweaks
M4	Data collection (Wave 1)
M5	Data collection (Wave 2)
M6	Cleaning & analysis begins

Step 4: Anticipate and Mitigate Risks

Research rarely goes exactly to plan. Proactively identify risks and draft mitigation strategies.

Risk	Mitigation
Low response rate	Use incentives, send 2–3 reminders
Ambiguous questionnaire items	Pilot with think-aloud protocol
Attrition between waves	Collect email for follow-up, offer continuity bonus
TikTok access changes (e.g., bans)	Broaden platform list, add contingency questions

Step 5: Create the Methodology Skeleton

Draft the outline of your methods chapter with headings and short bullets beneath each. Here's a recommended structure:

1. **Research Design**
   - Longitudinal, quantitative survey
2. **Participants & Sampling**
   - 200 undergraduates; stratified recruitment
3. **Measures**
   - GAD-7, social media frequency scale
4. **Procedure**
   - Online survey; 2 waves; IRB consent
5. **Data Analysis Plan**
   - Regression; change scores; SPSS
6. **Ethical Considerations**
   - IRB details; digital privacy
7. **Timeline & Resources**
   - Gantt chart; software needs; assistants

Save this file under your research folder as Methodology_Chapter_Outline.docx.

Final Tips: Staying on Track

- **Meet with your advisor**: Book a 15-minute check-in this week to review your outline.
- **Keep documents versioned**: Back up your plan with timestamps.

- **Document assumptions**: If you're unsure about sample size or methods, flag those questions for further reading or supervisor input.

Sprint Task

Task	Output
Create your full methodology skeleton	.docx or .md file
Build a one-page Gantt chart	Inserted into draft or exported as PDF
List IRB components (instruments, forms)	Checklist ready for submission
Identify two major risks and fixes	Bullet point plan
Schedule advisor review	Email confirmation or meeting booked

Reflection Prompt:

What part of your design feels most solid—and which part still feels vulnerable? Note one strength you're proud of and one question you need help resolving.

Next Steps

Next, in Day 28, we'll shift focus to self-reflection and resilience. You've been building your literature review and research plan over four intense weeks—Day 28 will offer tools to reflect, reset, and strengthen your mindset for the chapters ahead.

You now hold a research-ready blueprint in your hands. Chapter 3 is already half-written. Stay steady—you're doing extraordinary work.

Day 27 Summary Box

- Today marks the pivot from synthesizing existing research to planning how you'll generate your own—drafting the structural blueprint of your methodology chapter.
- Anchor your design to your **research question and literature gap**, using the bridge paragraph from Day 26 to maintain alignment and logic.
- Build a **detailed outline** including key components: participants, instruments, procedures, analysis plan, and ethical safeguards.

- Create a **Gap–Method Matrix** and **Gantt chart** to clarify how your study will unfold and how each method responds to your identified gap.
- Plan practical logistics: IRB approval, pilot testing, recruitment, and risk mitigation strategies (e.g., attrition, low response rate).
- Draft and save your **Methodology Chapter Skeleton** to structure your next steps with confidence.

Day 28: Managing Time and Staying Motivated

After completing a major intellectual task like a full literature review chapter, it's tempting to pause for too long—or, worse, to lose momentum entirely. But Day 28 invites a different response: one that blends rest, reflection, and deliberate forward planning.

This chapter is about you—the researcher behind the research. By now, you've proven your ability to work consistently, think critically, and produce substantial academic writing. What lies ahead—data collection, analysis, and subsequent chapters—requires just as much focus and emotional energy. To stay the course, you'll need a framework for managing your time, preserving your motivation, and maintaining balance. You don't need superhuman stamina—you need strategy.

Recognizing the Win

Before rushing ahead, take a moment to recognize what you've done. You've completed a structured literature review—a task that many students find overwhelming or never fully finish. Acknowledge that win. Write it down, say it aloud, or share it with a peer.

Small celebrations reinforce progress. Dopamine research shows that marking milestones builds motivational momentum (Harvard Summer School, 2023).

Write down a sentence that connects your research to your deeper "why." Tape it to your wall or make it your screensaver.

"I want to understand how social platforms affect students' well-being so I can design better digital environments."

Building a Realistic Roadmap

Without structure, ambition quickly becomes overwhelm. You don't need to see the whole staircase—just the next step. Break your remaining thesis work into manageable blocks using weekly and monthly planning.

Use Gantt or Kanban Boards

Visual project management tools like Trello, Notion, or simple Excel Gantt charts help break work into visible chunks. Don't overplan—focus on *this month.*

Example – 4-week Sprint Schedule

- *Week 1:* Finalize survey + IRB submission
- *Week 2:* Pilot test survey + adjustments
- *Week 3:* Launch data collection
- *Week 4:* Begin analysis framework setup

Apply the Time Box Strategy

Parkinson's Law reminds us: "Work expands to fill the time allotted." To beat this trap, *constrain* your tasks. Use time boxing: assign fixed time blocks to tasks (e.g., "9–10 a.m. write 1 intro paragraph"). Short bursts of focus often outperform long unstructured days.

Tip: Pair time boxing with the *Pomodoro Technique*—25 minutes of deep work followed by a 5-minute break. Repeat four times, then take a longer break.

Routines That Replenish, Not Drain

You're not a writing machine—you're a cognitive athlete. Like athletes, researchers need cycles of effort and recovery. A growing body of literature shows that short movement breaks during writing blocks improve executive function and cognitive stamina.

Try this: After every 2 Pomodoro cycles, walk for 5 minutes outdoors or do light stretching. It's not procrastination—it's brain fuel.

Also, be honest about burnout risks. Incorporate non-screen time: hobbies, exercise, music, nature. No one writes well from exhaustion.

Build Support Systems

You don't have to do this alone. External accountability improves completion rates across thesis programs globally. That doesn't mean hiring a coach—it means finding a peer, forming a writing group, or using a virtual co-working tool.

Options:

- **Peer check-in**: Message a classmate each week to share goals
- **Focusmate**: Join virtual writing sessions with real accountability (90% task completion rate reported)
- **Writing center hours**: Schedule office hours with tutors or academic writing advisors

Tech Tools That Help (and When to Use Them)

Need	Tool	Best Use
Task tracking & planning	Notion "Thesis Planner" template	Weekly/monthly sprint scheduling
Time management	Forest, Pomofocus, Focus To-Do	Pomodoro sessions; visual work-break rhythm
Visual project tracking	Trello / Gantt chart in Excel	Task timelines with status updates
Focus / accountability	Focusmate	Co-working sessions to prevent drift

Daily Motivation Habits

1. **Morning mantra**: Start each workday by reading your "why" sentence aloud.
2. **Micro-goal setting**: Define 1–2 specific tasks *you can complete today.*
3. **End-of-day review**: Note one thing you did well, no matter how small.

These practices build resilience and cultivate self-compassion—a key trait in students who persist despite stress or setbacks (Self-Compassion.org research).

Sample Weekly Plan (With Rewards)

Day	Main Task	Time Box	Reward
Monday	Finalize survey questions	2 × 25 min Pomodoros	Coffee at favorite café
Tuesday	Draft IRB form	3 × 25 min	20 min walk in the park
Wednesday	Meet supervisor, adjust survey	2 × 30 min revisions	Watch a documentary episode
Thursday	Outline analysis strategy	2 × 25 min	30 min creative hobby session
Friday	Catch-up buffer + light reading	1 focused hour	Early log off + lunch with friend

Sprint Task – Your One Week Action Plan

1. **Map your next 5–7 days**
   – List 3–5 specific, achievable thesis tasks (e.g., revise survey, read 3 methods papers).
2. **Time box each task**
   – Schedule at least one 25-minute Pomodoro for each major task.
3. **Choose a reward**
   – Assign a treat for completing the toughest task (movie, walk, snack, anything you enjoy).
4. **Set accountability**
   – Book one writing session with a peer or schedule a Focusmate slot.
5. **Write your purpose mantra**
   – One sentence explaining why your research matters *to you*. Post it somewhere visible.

Sample Affirmations

"I don't need to write everything today—I only need to take one step."
"My research can help others understand what I once found confusing."
"Consistency beats perfection."

Final Thoughts

Day 28 is not about academic writing—it's about the writer. By adopting sustainable work patterns and renewing your internal motivation, you're building not just a thesis, but a capacity for long-term intellectual endurance.

You've already accomplished something extraordinary. Now, give yourself the tools to keep going—steadily, thoughtfully, and with self-compassion.

Day 28 Summary Box

- Today shifts focus from the writing itself to you—the researcher—by helping you manage energy, motivation, and planning for the work ahead.
- Acknowledge the milestone you've reached: completing a structured, scholarly literature review. Celebrate this progress to reinforce motivation.
- Reconnect with your purpose by writing a **personal "why" statement**—a reminder of the deeper impact behind your research.
- Use simple planning tools like **Gantt charts, Trello, or Notion** to break your upcoming thesis work into manageable weekly sprints.
- Apply **time-boxing** and the **Pomodoro Technique** to improve focus and prevent burnout. Pair deep work with rest cycles for sustained cognitive energy.
- Create systems of **support and accountability** through writing peers, virtual co-working (e.g., Focusmate), or check-ins with advisors.
- Build a weekly habit loop: **micro-goal setting**, **scheduled rewards**, and **end-of-day reflections** to maintain momentum and protect mental well-being.

Day 29: Final Review and Submission Preparation

You've come a long way. From refining research questions to synthesizing the literature and articulating the gap your study will fill, your Chapter 2—the Literature Review—is now near completion. But Day 29 reminds us that scholarly writing is judged not only by its ideas, but also by the clarity, consistency, and professionalism of its presentation.

This final stage isn't about deep revision—it's about final refinement. Like proofreading a journal article before sending it off for publication, your job now is to inspect every detail that could distract a reviewer from engaging with your argument. Done well, this final review will showcase your intellectual precision and set the tone for what comes next.

1. Run a "Whole Chapter Flight Check"

Final Front-to-Back Read

Even after multiple edits, a last silent read of your full chapter can catch surprising issues: repeated phrases, awkward transitions, orphaned headings, or citation inconsistencies. If possible, print it out—on-paper proofreading continues to outperform on-screen editing in spotting minor errors (Cambridge Assessment, 2022).

Look especially for:

- Unnecessary repetition ("social media platforms" repeated three times in a paragraph).
- Connective phrases missing from new transitions.
- Any leftover tracked changes or comment bubbles.

Verify Template Compliance

Your university may have strict formatting rules—don't overlook them. Match every page margin, heading level, and font style to your institution's official template. Confirm the presence and formatting of:

- Chapter title page (e.g., "Chapter 2: Literature Review").
- Running headers (if required).
- Page numbers (usually bottom center or top right).

Tip: The UNC Graduate School specifies 1-inch margins, double spacing, and bold, title case for level 1 headings.

Reference List Integrity

Use Zotero or another reference manager's "refresh" function, then run a final citation checker (such as Recite) to confirm:

- Every in-text citation is included in the reference list—and vice versa.
- All entries are formatted per style guide (e.g., APA 7: italics for journal titles, sentence case for article titles).
- Hanging indents are applied correctly.

Professional proofreaders warn that mispunctuated references are among the most common last-minute errors (Dissertation by Design, 2022).

2. Prepare Supplementary Elements (If Required)

Some departments or submission portals ask for materials beyond the chapter itself. Prepare these now:

Item	Required When?	Notes
Abstract & Keywords	If each chapter needs one (APA: ≤250 words)	Write in present tense, include 4–6 keywords
Figure/Table Captions	If figures/tables are included	Numbered (e.g., Figure 1: Sample Flow), cited in-text
Placeholders	For chapters not yet written	Insert pages titled "Chapter 3 Begins" or "To be completed" as needed

3. Lock Down File Integrity

File Naming

Use a version-controlled naming convention that's clear and timestamped:

2025_05_29_LitReview_FINAL_YourLastName.docx

Also export a clean PDF version and lock it (to prevent further accidental edits). Save both formats.

Backup Strategy

Follow the 3–2–1 rule:

- **3** copies (your working file, a backup, and a submission copy)
- **2** cloud services (e.g., Google Drive + Dropbox)
- **1** external device (e.g., USB or hard drive)

This guards against sync errors, accidental deletions, and local drive crashes.

4. Draft a Professional Submission Email

Your submission note doesn't need to be lengthy, but it should be courteous, clear, and informative.

Example Email (Template)

Subject: Chapter 2 – Literature Review Final Draft for Review

Body:
Dear [Supervisor's Name],

Please find attached the final draft of Chapter 2: Literature Review. I have incorporated your earlier feedback, including:

- Strengthening the discussion of platform comparisons in Section 2.3
- Clarifying the transition to the methodology in the conclusion
- Correcting reference formatting per APA guidelines

The document follows our department's formatting template. I'm happy to make any further adjustments as needed.

Best regards,
[Your Name]

Always triple-check the filename and attachment before sending.

5. Final Checklist

Before you hit send, confirm each of the following:

☑	Task
✓	Full read-through completed (printed or PDF)
✓	Chapter title page formatted (e.g., "Chapter 2: Literature Review")
✓	Margins, spacing, and font comply with department requirements
✓	All in-text citations matched in reference list; Recite cross-check passed
✓	Figures and tables are numbered, cited, and captioned
✓	Abstract and keywords added (if required)
✓	File named clearly; final copy saved as locked PDF
✓	File backed up to cloud and external drive
✓	Submission email written and queued

6. Reflect and Release

You've done more than write a chapter—you've engaged critically with a body of scholarship, sharpened your thinking, and prepared a document that reflects your capabilities as a researcher. Before you move on, pause and write a one-line reflection about what you've gained.

"I now understand how to frame and defend a research gap with confidence."
"I've learned to manage a major writing project without burnout."

Small reflections like these mark psychological progress as well as academic milestones.

Sprint Task – Submission Ready

#	Task	Evidence
1	Final minor tweaks	Corrected any remaining errors (e.g., page numbers, mis-capitalization)
2	Backup files	PDF and Word versions saved to cloud + external device
3	Compose submission email	Written using template and sent/queued
4	Write 50-word reflection	Journal or email note documenting biggest learning point
5	Celebrate	Treat yourself—a short walk, favorite snack, or relaxing activity

Final Words

You've now produced a ready-to-submit literature review chapter that is thorough, polished, and institutionally compliant. This is a major scholarly milestone—whether this chapter stands alone or anchors your full thesis.

Day 29 Summary Box

- Today is dedicated to finalizing and submitting your literature review chapter—not rewriting, but perfecting presentation, formatting, and submission readiness.
- Conduct a **whole-chapter read-through** (ideally in print or PDF) to catch leftover errors, repeated phrases, or formatting inconsistencies.
- Confirm your manuscript **complies fully with your institution's formatting requirements**: margins, spacing, heading levels, title pages, and page numbers.
- Run a **reference integrity check** using Zotero or Recite to ensure that every in-text citation is matched, properly formatted, and included in your reference list.
- Prepare any **required supplementary items** like chapter abstracts, figure/table captions, or placeholder pages for upcoming chapters.
- **Finalize and version your files** using clear, timestamped naming conventions. Export a clean PDF and back up all versions using the 3–2–1 rule (3 copies, 2 clouds, 1 device).
- Draft and send a **professional submission email** that outlines what was revised, confirms formatting, and invites further feedback.

Day 30: Reflection and Next Steps

Congratulations—Day 30 marks the completion of your literature review sprint and the beginning of a new, more empowered phase of your thesis journey. Today is about pausing with purpose. Rather than pushing into the next task, take this day to consolidate your progress, recognize your achievement, and chart a thoughtful path forward. You've not only written a fully developed literature review chapter—you've also built habits, tools, and workflows that will serve you through to submission and beyond.

Celebrate the Win: Acknowledge What You've Done

It's easy to finish a major task and immediately rush toward the next. Resist that urge. Academic research is intellectually demanding, emotionally taxing, and often solitary. Taking time to celebrate what you've accomplished is not a luxury—it's fuel for sustainable motivation.

Try this:

List three things you can now do better than you could 30 days ago. For example:

- Search academic databases more strategically.
- Use Zotero to generate a formatted bibliography in seconds.
- Structure a literature review paragraph using the PEEL method.

Post these on your wall or planner. Let them remind you that you are a capable, growing scholar.

"I now know how to track a research gap from keyword to question to method."
"I wrote, formatted, and finalized a full chapter—start to finish."
"I've built a system I can use again for Chapter 3."

According to educational psychology studies, celebrating small wins stimulates dopamine production and reinforces learning behavior (University of Minnesota Extension, 2022).

Reflect on What You Learned

Structured reflection turns experience into insight. Consider the strategies, tools, and habits that made this sprint successful.

Journal Prompt 1: What Worked?

- Did a daily writing schedule help?
- Was the Pomodoro method effective?
- Did accountability check-ins or Focusmate keep you consistent?

Journal Prompt 2: What Surprised You?

- Was there a part of the chapter you thought would be harder than it was?
- Did AI tools (e.g., ChatGPT, Recite, Paperpal) help more than expected?

Journal Prompt 3: What Would You Improve Next Time?

- Would earlier outlining have helped?
- Did you underestimate how long formatting would take?

"I didn't expect reverse outlining to be so powerful in spotting weak structure." *"Grammarly caught more issues than I thought—but I still needed to read out loud."*

Reflection builds metacognition, which is one of the strongest predictors of writing quality and academic self-efficacy (ResearchGate, 2023).

Plan What Comes Next

The literature review is a keystone chapter—but now your focus shifts to methodology, data collection, and analysis. With the momentum of the past 30 days, Day 30 is the perfect time to sketch a practical roadmap for the next phase.

Macro Timeline Snapshot

Month	Milestone	Tools & Notes
1	Finalize survey & IRB docs	Notion board, advisor review
2–3	Pilot and data collection	Qualtrics, Focusmate, consent forms
4	Preliminary analysis	SPSS/R, weekly writing sessions
5	Draft methods & results	Pomodoro + SMART micro goals

Micro Goal Example (Next 7 Days)

- ☑ Monday: Refine survey items.
- ☑ Tuesday: Draft IRB rationale.
- ☑ Wednesday: Review consent script.
- ☑ Friday: Submit IRB packet.

Remember to apply **SMART goal principles**—specific, measurable, attainable, relevant, and time-bound.

Sustain Motivation Through Structure and Support

Now that you've proven you can work with consistency and depth, maintain that discipline by building support into your next stage.

Tips for Momentum:

- Join or form a **Writing Accountability Group (WAG)**.
- Schedule **Focusmate** sessions or peer check-ins.
- Build a **Kanban board** with "To Do / Doing / Done" columns for visual tracking.
- Include **mindfulness breaks** and offline activities to prevent burnout.

A meta-analysis confirms that structured writing plans combined with wellness strategies increase graduate writing persistence (PubMed, 2023).

Sprint Task – Reflect, Reset, and Reboot

Step	Task	Output
1	Write a 150-word reflection	Journal entry or blog post
2	Set two SMART goals for the coming week	Note in planner or Notion
3	Plan a celebration activity	Calendar reminder
4	Schedule next writing session	Focusmate or WAG invite sent
5	Build a Kanban board for Chapter 3 tasks	Screenshot or link to Trello

Final Encouragement

You have just completed one of the most difficult chapters in any thesis—and you've done it in 30 focused, deliberate days. You now know how to plan, structure, and execute a major writing project using tools that amplify your strengths.

Keep moving forward, even if the pace varies. Keep celebrating each step. And keep remembering that what you're writing matters—not just for your thesis, but for the world of knowledge you're contributing to.

Day 30 Summary Box

- Today is a moment to **pause, celebrate, and reflect**. You've completed a full, submission-ready literature review chapter in just 30 days—a major academic milestone.
- Take time to **acknowledge your growth**: improved search strategies, writing workflows, and literature synthesis skills. Write down three things you can now do better than 30 days ago.
- Use **structured journaling prompts** to reflect on what worked, what surprised you, and what you'll improve in the next phase. This builds metacognitive awareness and academic confidence.
- Begin mapping the **next stage of your thesis**: finalizing your research instruments, submitting ethics applications, and outlining Chapter 3.
- Apply **SMART goals and micro-planning** to keep momentum. A simple weekly roadmap prevents overwhelm and maintains steady progress.
- Sustain motivation by setting up systems: Kanban boards, Focusmate sessions, accountability check-ins, and rest routines.

Concluding Remarks

You've reached the end of *Dissertation Literature Review Sprint* —not just a book, but a rigorous academic journey. Over the past thirty chapters, you've stepped through the entire process of building a literature review from the ground up: clarifying your research question, mapping the field, synthesizing sources, navigating contradictions, aligning your argument with methodological plans, and polishing the final product to submission standard. That is no small feat.

But more importantly, you've done something even rarer in the world of graduate research: you've learned how to *work deliberately, sustainably, and with strategic clarity*. You now possess not only a finished chapter but also a repeatable framework for tackling every phase of thesis writing—from methods to results to discussion and beyond.

You've acquired essential skills:

- How to translate a nebulous topic into a structured review with a clear gap.
- How to integrate AI tools, reference managers, and writing frameworks to speed up and improve your process.
- How to revise with rigor, format with precision, and present your work professionally.
- How to sustain momentum, manage time, and protect your wellbeing during high-stakes academic work.

This book was designed not just to help you finish one chapter, but to equip you with the mindset and tools of a capable, independent scholar. You've now seen what's possible when effort meets structure. You've seen what thirty days of focus can yield. The next time you sit down to write—whether it's a methodology chapter, a paper submission, or a funding proposal—you'll do so not with doubt, but with direction.

So take a moment. Breathe. Reflect. Be proud. And when you're ready, carry what you've built here into the next phase of your academic work.

You have momentum. You have mastery. And now, you have a blueprint.

Go write your future.

Ready to Go Deeper?

You've completed the *Dissertation Literature Review Sprint*—and now you're ready for what comes next.

The ***Dissertation Literature Review Sprint: The Guided Experience Course*** takes everything you've learned in this book and expands it into a live, guided experience. Inside, you'll find:

- Video walkthroughs for every step of the 30-day sprint
- Downloadable templates, citation workflows, and Zotero libraries
- Live Q&A and community accountability groups
- Personalized feedback on your literature review draft

Whether you're just starting or polishing your final draft, the course gives you expert support, real-time feedback, and the structure to finish strong.

👉 **Join the Waitlist** or **Sign Up Now** at:

https://www.gradsummit.com/dissertation-literature-review-sprint

Or scan the QR code below to save your spot now.

Mastering Research Series

This book is part of the *Mastering Research: Design, Execution, and Publishing Made Simple* series—an essential collection authored by Dr. Rafiq Muhammad. This all-in-one series offers step-by-step guidance, real-world strategies, and practical tools tailored for each stage of the research process. The series includes: **1. Research Design Simplified**, **2. Literature Review Simplified**, **3. Research Proposal Writing Simplified**, **4. Write and Publish Scientific Paper**, **5. PhD Journey Simplified**, and **6. Qualitative Data Analysis with ChatGPT and QualCoder**. Together, these books provide a complete roadmap—from formulating your first research question to confidently publishing your findings.

Literature Review Simplified: A Practical Guide for Beginners (Mastering Rese...

Buying Options

32

Literature Review Simplified: A Practical Guide for Beginners Second Edition ...

Buying Options

17

Research Design Simplified: A Beginner's Guide to Qualitative, Quantitative, ...

Buying Options

64

Write and Publish Scientific Paper: A Step-By-Step Publication Guide For Begi...

Buying Options

10

Research Proposal Writing Simplified: A Step-by-Step Guide to Research Propos...

Buying Options

7

Qualitative Data Analysis With Chatgpt And Qualcoder: A Step-By-Step Guide To...

Buying Options

14

Scan to order on Amazon

One Last Thing

If you found this book useful and enjoyed reading it, I would be grateful if you would post a review. Your support really makes a difference. I read all the reviews personally so I can receive your suggestions and make this book even better.

Thank you for your support!

References

1. Rafiq M. Literature Review Simplified: A Practical Guide for Beginners Second Edition. 2024.
2. Cooper H. The Handbook of Research Synthesis and Meta-Analysis. 2009.
3. Wyborn C, Louder E, Harrison J, Montambault J, Montana J, Ryan M, et al. Understanding the Impacts of Research Synthesis. Environ Sci Policy [Internet]. 2018 Aug;86:72–84. Available from: https://linkinghub.elsevier.com/retrieve/pii/S1462901117311048
4. Rafiq Muhammad. Literature Review Simplified: A Practical Guide for Beginners Second Edition. 2024.
5. Perplexity AI [AI-powered search engine]. Perplexity AI, Inc. [Internet]. 2025 [cited 2025 May 31]. Available from: https://www.perplexity.ai/
6. Consensus: AI-powered Academic Search Engine. Consensus AI [Internet]. 2025 [cited 2025 May 31]. Available from: https://consensus.app/
7. ResearchRabbit: AI-driven Literature Discovery and Visualization Tool. ResearchRabbit Technologies [Internet]. 2025 [cited 2025 May 31]. Available from: https://www.researchrabbit.ai/
8. Connected Papers: A visual tool to help researchers find and explore academic papers. Connected Papers [Internet]. 2025 [cited 2025 May 31]. Available from: https://www.connectedpapers.com/
9. Elicit: The AI Research Assistant. Elicit [Internet]. 2025 [cited 2025 May 31]. Available from: https://elicit.com/
10. Scholarcy: AI-powered research summarization tool. Scholarcy [Internet]. 2025 [cited 2025 May 31]. Available from: https://www.scholarcy.com/
11. Zotero: Free easy to use reference management tool. Zotero [Internet]. 2025 [cited 2025 May 31]. Available from: https://www.zotero.org/
12. Scite: A smart citation index that displays the context of citations and classifies their intent using deep learning. Scite [Internet]. 2025 [cited 2025 May 31]. Available from: https://scite.ai/
13. ChatGPT: Generative AI chatbot [AI-powered chatbot and research tool]. OpenAI [Internet]. 2025 [cited 2025 May 31]. Available from: https://chatgpt.com/
14. Claude: AI assistant. Anthropic [Internet]. 2025 [cited 2025 May 31]. Available from: https://www.anthropic.com/claude
15. Cooke A, Smith D, Booth A. Beyond PICO: The SPIDER Tool for Qualitative Evidence Synthesis. Qual Health Res [Internet]. 2012 Oct 24;22(10):1435–43. Available from: http://journals.sagepub.com/doi/10.1177/1049732312452938

16. A Research Framework. FINER [Internet]. 2025 [cited 2025 May 31]. Available from: https://scientific-publishing.webshop.elsevier.com/research-process/finer-research-framework/
17. an R package to facilitate quasi-automatic search strategy development for systematic reviews. litsearchr [Internet]. 2025 [cited 2025 May 31]. Available from: https://elizagrames.github.io/litsearchr/
18. TextRazor: AI-powered Natural Language Processing API. TextRazor [Internet]. 2025 [cited 2025 May 31]. Available from: https://www.textrazor.com/
19. Ouzzani M, Hammady H, Fedorowicz Z, Elmagarmid A. Rayyan—a web and mobile app for systematic reviews. Syst Rev. 2016 Dec 5;5(1):210.
20. Litmaps: AI-powered literature discovery and visualization tool. Litmaps [Internet]. 2024 [cited 2025 May 31]. Available from: https://www.litmaps.com/
21. Centre for Science and Technology Studies LU. VOSviewer: software for constructing and visualizing bibliometric networks [Internet]. 2025 [cited 2025 May 31]. Available from: https://www.vosviewer.com/
22. InfraNodus: AI-powered text network visualization tool. Nodus Labs (InfraNodus SAS). [Internet]. 2025 [cited 2025 May 31]. Available from: https://infranodus.com/
23. Purdue OWL W and HU. Writing a Literature Review [Internet]. 2025 [cited 2025 May 31]. Available from: https://owl.purdue.edu/owl/research_and_citation/conducting_research/writing_a_literature_review.html
24. University of Staffordshire. PEEL Paragraphs [Internet]. 2024 [cited 2025 May 31]. Available from: https://libguides.staffs.ac.uk/academic_writing/PEEL
25. University of West London. Writing Critical Paragraphs: Topic, Expand, Evidence, Explanation [Internet]. 2025 [cited 2025 May 31]. Available from: https://www.uwl.ac.uk/current-students/support-students/study-support/writing-critical-paragraphs
26. Purdue OWL. Paraphrase: Write It in Your Own Words [Internet]. 2025 [cited 2025 May 31]. Available from: https://owl.purdue.edu/owl/research_and_citation/using_research/quoting_paraphrasing_and_summarizing/paraphrasing.html

Made in the USA
Monee, IL
02 March 2026